Quickstart in C++

William B. Jones
California State University Dominguez Hills

Scott/Jones Inc.
Publishers
P. O. Box 696
El Granada, CA 94018
(415) 726-2436
(415) 726-4693 (FAX)

Quickstart in C++
William B. Jones

ISBN 1-881991-38-5

Text Design and Composition: William B. Jones
Book Manufacturing: Malloy Lithographing, Inc.

V W X Y Z   5 6 7 8

Additional titles of interest from Scott/Jones

C by Discovery, 2nd ed. (emphasizing ANSI C), by L. S. Foster

Assembly Language for the IBM PC Family, revised 1995, by William B. Jones

Quickstart in Windows and **The Windows Textbook**, by Stewart Venit

Quick Start in DOS and **The DOS-6 Coursebook**, by Forest Lin

The Visual BASIC Coursebook, by Forest Lin

FORTRAN for Engineers, 2nd ed., by Gary Bronson

Modern FORTRAN 77/90: Alternate Edition, by Gary Bronson

Computer Architecture and Assembly Language: The MC68000, by G. M. Prabhu and Charles Wright

WordPerfect for Windows, by Rolayne Day

Table of Contents

For Jacqueline, who makes everything possible

Preface

The C++ language is (almost) an extension of the C language. The purposes of the extension were to make C safer, more expressive, and most importantly, give it a powerful object-oriented programming capability. (The word 'almost' is used in the first sentence because C++ makes minor changes to C as well as extending it.)

Purpose and Organization

The purpose of this book is to give the reader a quick introduction to the most important features of the C++ language. To do this, I have attempted to avoid anything that is not of central importance and as far as possible, to steer you away from the rather sizable swamps that abound in the language. Chapters 1–5 give a basic introduction to C++ and the class concept, which is fundamental to C++ and object-oriented programming. There isn't much point in covering less than these. Chapter 8 introduces destructors and more advanced concepts of constructors, and Chapter 9 discusses class hierarchy and virtual functions. Chapters 7 and 10 give substantial examples of object-oriented programming and Chapter 8 and an extended example in Chapter 6 show how classes can be used to represent abstract data types. A diagram of chapter dependencies appears at the end of this preface.

At various times in this book we will indicate especially important statements visually. We will note Rules

▌ This is a Rule, an absolute requirement of the C++ language.

and Rules of Thumb

RULE *of 7*

‖ This is a Rule of Thumb, which is not a requirement of C++
‖ but which your author thinks you should follow
‖ nonetheless.

Assumed background
What isn't covered

The book assumes that the reader knows or is learning C, which is not covered here. There is, however, a cross-reference to four C textbooks in an appendix.

In order to compress a very large and unruly language within a hundred pages or so, I have had to omit a great number of topics. Some, such as `const`, are in my opinion examples of good ideas gone wrong. (In my experience, `const` declarations add no substantial safety, and the difficulty in understanding a C++ program is directly proportional to the number of `const` declarations that occur.) I have also omitted things like the `struct` version of classes, which seems redundant, and `friend` functions, which seem of only minor use at the level of difficulty I get to here. More serious omissions are topics such as templates and exception handling. Both of these topics are very important but the former is notationally messy and adding both would have greatly increased the length of the book. I have also avoided lots of rules, like how particular examples of overloaded functions work. I have tried to warn the prospective user and give a few techniques of experimental computer science that may help in cases of difficulty.

Speaking of experimental computer science, whereas C is a rather small, elegant language, C++ is an enormous irregular sprawl that grows and changes with each new version. It has not yet been standardized, and it doesn't seem likely to me that it ever will be satisfactorily. As a result, frequent experimentation is often the best approach to understanding how the language works.

Unfortunately, what one quickly discovers is that what works in one C++ may fail miserably in another, as the following example demonstrates. The example given here can be understood as an object lesson in the vagaries of various C++ implementations without understanding the C++ involved. The details of the C++ can be found in Chapters 2 (reference parameters) and 6 (classes).

A Cautionary Tale

One way in which C++ extends C is to add the reference parameters, *a la* var parameters in Pascal and inout parameters in Ada. These can be used when a function needs to change the value of one of its parameters more than locally. Where the Pascal programmer would write

```
procedure proc( var I : integer );
begin
    ... I := 14; ...
end ;
```

the C++ programmer could write

```
void proc( int &I )
{
    .... I = 14; ...
}
```

To guarantee safe use of **var** parameters, Pascal requires that the actual parameters corresponding to them be variables. C++ as expected takes a looser approach. Thus sometimes in this situation non-variable actual parameters can be cast to be variables, and in some C++s, this is even done automatically, passing pointers to automatically created temporaries. We have the following situation in three different versions of C++:

```
class INT {
   public:
      int i;
      INT( int I ) { i = I; }
      INT operator +( INT j ) { return INT(i + j.i); }
};

void rIPar( INT &i ) {}

void riPar( int &i ) {}

void IPar ( INT  i ) {}

void main( void )
{
   INT i = 22;
//                                   Borland C++    Visual C++    GNU C++
   rIPar( INT(14) );  //                OK             OK            OK
   rIPar( INT(i+1) ); //                OK             Warning       Error
```

The C++ Lottery

```
        rIPar( 14 );        //    Warning     Error      OK
        rIPar( i+1 );       //      OK       Warning      OK
        riPar( int(14) );   //    Warning     Error      OK
        riPar( 14 );        //    Warning     Error      OK
        IPar ( 14 );        //      OK         OK         OK
    }
```

(Where warnings occur, the code seems to compile 'correctly'. The error under GNU C++ is probably a bug.) As you can see, experiment is necessary, but not necessarily sufficient!

All programs in this book have been tested, where appropriate, with Borland C++ version 4.0 and Visual C++ Professional version 1.0 on a 33 MHz 486 PC and with GNU C++ version 2.2.2 on a DEC VAX 3300 running Ultrix. The resulting programs and makefiles for their creation are available on the disk that accompanies this book.

What I used to write it

This book was typeset by the author, *painfully*, using Microsoft Word 6.0 with illustrations also by the author done with Adobe Illustrator 5.5, both on various models of Macintosh computers. Fonts used are Baskerville MT, Franklin Gothic No. 2, Courier, and Tekton. The screen snapshot of a Mandelbrot set was made and converted to PostScript using HiJaac Pro on the 486. Camera-ready copy was produced on a HP LaserJet 4MP.

Who helped

Even a book as small as this one is the work of many hands. I would like to thank the following for reading and commenting on various versions of the text.

Stephen Allan
Utah State University

Ken Collier
Northern Arizona State University

Rod Farcas
Community College of Allegheny County

Frank Paiano
Southwestern College

Wang-Chan Wong
California State University Dominguez Hills

Wayne Carulo
Red Rocks Community College

Bill Davis
Gaston College

Christopher Haynes
Indiana University

Brenda Sonderegger
Montana State University

Guy Zimmerman
Bowling Green State University

Brenda Sonderegger also class tested a version. I would like to thank my publisher, Richard Jones (no relation), for teaching me a great deal about how to write a textbook. And finally, I would like to thank Emily Dickinson for occasional inspiration. Only I am to blame for any insufficiencies in all that help.

Bill Jones
Hermosa Beach, California, 1995
wbj@dhvx20.csudh.edu

Chapter Dependencies

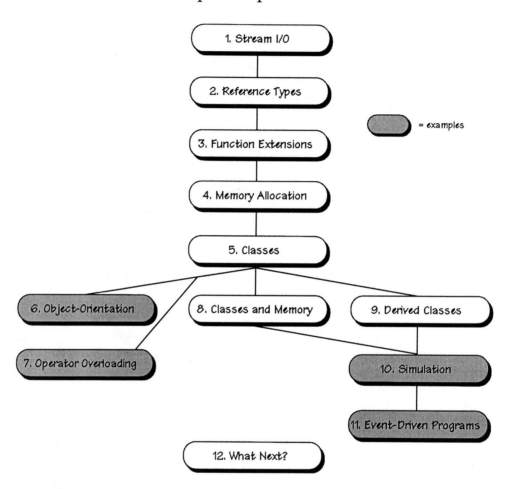

1. Getting Started with C++

1.1 A Simple Program

Turning an ANSI C program into a C++ program is easy. If you have included prototypes for all the functions you use (which you should do anyway), all you have to do is change the extension on the file name. C++ compilers generally require an extension such as .C, .cxx, or .cpp to indicate that the program is C++ code. We will use .cpp where appropriate. Header files still use the extension .h. Thus the ubiquitous C hello program

```
/* hello.c -- say hello to the world */

#include <stdio.h>

void main( void )
{
    printf("Hello, world!\n");
}
```

becomes the potentially equally ubiquitous C++ hello program:

new comment

```
// hello.cpp -- say hello to the world

#include <stdio.h>

void main( void )
{
    printf("Hello, world!\n");
}
```

simply by changing the file name from hello.c to hello.cpp. We have also used a second form of **comment** allowed by C++. At any time, the appearance of '//' indicates that the rest of the line is a comment. For example,

```
x = 5;      // this is a comment
```

(Some C compilers now also allow this notation.)

1.2 Stream I/O

Even in a simple program like hello.cpp, C++ can make our lives easier in various ways. C++ has a style of I/O, called **stream I/O**, which is much easier to use than printf in simple situations. It also avoids errors that are easy to make with printf. The following is a version of the hello program using these new ideas:

1

```
// hello2.cpp -- say hello to the world

#include <iostream.h>

void main( void )
{
    cout << "Hello, world!" << endl;
}
```

new comment

The actual output is performed by the statement

easy output:
cout

```
cout << "Hello, world!" << endl;
```

This statement is interpreted as first sending the string `"Hello, world!"`, then an end-of-line, to the output stream `cout`, which is the user's display screen. The statement can be read 'cout **gets** `"Hello, world!"`, **then** `endl`.' It is equivalent

end output lines
with endl

to

```
cout << "Hello, world!";
cout << endl ;
```

and to

```
cout << "Hello, world!\n";
```

Stream I/O can be intermixed with traditional C I/O (e.g., `printf`) as long as stream and traditional I/O generate separate lines of output.

For a more elaborate example, consider

```
// add1.cpp -- add two numbers

#include <iostream.h>

void main( void )
{
    cout << "The sum of " << 3 << " and " << 5 << " is " << 3 + 5
       << endl;
}
```

which produces the line of output

```
The sum of 3 and 5 is 8
```

You can think of the 'cout `<<...`' statement as marching across the page, specifying the output fields in order:

```
cout << "The sum of " << 3 << " and " << 5 << " is " << 8;



              The sum of 3 and 5 is 8
```

One can also do input from the keyboard using the stream `cin`. The statement

```
cin >> a >> b >> c;
```

(read 'cin **gives** a **then** b **then** c') reads values for the variables a, b, and c from the keyboard. The values must be separated by blanks or ends of lines. Note that the traditional C version of this statement would be

```
scanf( "%d %d %d", &a, &b, &c );
```

If some of the ampersands (&) were missing, C would not detect this fact. When using `cin` in C++, ampersands are not required (or allowed).

The following is a variation of the adding program using input:

```
// add2.cpp -- add two numbers

#include <iostream.h>

void main( void )
{
   int a, b;

   cout << "Type in two integers ";
   cin >> a >> b;
   cout << "The sum of " << a << " and " << b << " is " << a + b
           << endl;
}
```

A sample run of add2 (user input in **boldface**) is

```
Type in two integers 23 44
The sum of 23 and 44 is 67
```

Unlike `scanf`, `cin` will also read octal and hexadecimal numbers when typed in the usual C format. Consider the following execution of add2:

```
Type in two numbers 023 0x44
The sum of 19 and 68 is 87
```

(The leading '0' in 023 indicates that the number is in octal, base 8, and the leading '0x' in 0x44 indicates that the number is in hex (hexadecimal, base 16).)

It is also possible to have `cin` interpret numbers as octal or hex numbers without requiring the user to type the leading '0' or '0x'. Each stream has a **current base** that is decimal (initially), octal, or hex. The base of a stream is changed by feeding it one of the string manipulators `dec`, `oct`, or `hex`, to change the base to decimal, octal, or hex, respectively. For instance,

change default
number base in
I/O with hex, oct,
and dec

```
// basein.cpp -- experiment with number bases and cin

#include <iostream.h>

void main( void )
{
   int a, b, c;

   cout << "Enter one number in octal, then two in hex: ";
   cin >> oct >> a >> hex >> b;
   cin >> c;
   cout << "The numbers are " << a << ", " << b << ", and " << c
          << endl;
}
```

can produce the run

```
Enter one number in octal, two in hex: 23 44 ab
The numbers are 19, 68, and 171
```

The use of two separate `cin` statements in the program above shows that the current base of `cin` is remembered from one call to the next.

The same technique can also be used to change the base in which numbers are output:

```
// baseout.cpp -- changing number bases in cout

#include <iostream.h>

void main( void )
{
   int a;

   cout << "Enter a number: ";
   cin >> a;
   cout << a << " = 0" << oct << a << " = 0x" << hex << a <<
endl;
}
```

A sample run is

```
Enter a number: 123
123 = 0173 = 0x7b
```

Use of stream I/O is especially nice when mixing numbers of different types and sizes. Using `scanf` and `printf`, you can get quite strange results if the type or size specified in the format string doesn't agree with that of the variable coming in or expression going out. When stream I/O is used in C++, all of this is taken care of for you automatically. For instance,

```
// types.cpp -- different data types and sizes using stream I/O

#include <iostream.h>

void main( void )
{
   int i;
   long int l;   // (possibly) longer than an integer
   char c;       // generally shorter than an int
   float f;      // number with a decimal point
   double d;     // number with dec. pt. and more digits

   cin >> i >> l >> c >> f >> d;
   cout << i << " " << l << " " << c << " " << f << " " << d <<
endl;
}
```

can produce the run

123 123456# 3.1415926535 3.1415926535
123 123456 # 3.141593 3.141593

Cin skips over white space (blanks, etc.) to arrive at the next input item. Thus the input line above could just as well have been typed

123   123456   #3.1415926535   3.1415926535

The extra digits of precision are saved in d. Cout in the default form used here just doesn't display them. As an example of the formatting decisions made by C++ stream I/O, consider the program

```
// float.cpp -- examples of output of float numbers with cout

#include <iostream.h>

void main( void )
{
   cout << 123.0 << endl;
   cout << 0.00123 << endl;
   cout << 1.2300 << endl;
   cout << 123000000000000000.0 << endl;
   cout << 0.000000000000000123 << endl;
}
```

which produces the output

```
123
0.00123
```

```
1.23
1.23e+17
1.23e-16
```

It is possible to change this default behavior and control output to a greater degree than `printf` using functions in the include file `iomanip.h`. However, I don't advise it. Simple stream I/O is a pleasure to use, but the fancy stuff is poorly designed, irregular, and not fun at all. I think you are better off using `printf` or other C functions if you want to do anything fancier than we have done here.

RULE of 9

> In C, the `char` data type only determines the size of memory allocated. In all other ways, a `char` is identical to a (signed or unsigned) `int`. In C++, a `char` stays a `char` until it is used in a non-trivial expression, which forces it to be an `int`.

Stream I/O demonstrates this difference. In C,

```
char c;
...
c = 'A' + 1;     // = 66
printf( "%d %c %d %c\n", 'A' + 1, 'A' + 1, c, c );
```

produces the output

```
66 B 66 B
```

In C++ though, the code

in C++, char is a real data type

```
char c;
...
c = 66;     // = 'A' + 1
cout << 'A' + 1 << " " << c << " " << c + 1 << endl;
```

produces the output

```
66 B 67
```

Of course in C++, we can use **type casting** to get any interpretation we want.

```
cout << (char) ('A' + 1) << " " << (int) c << " "
      << (char) (c + 1);
```

produces the output

```
B 66 C
```

Neither C nor C++ can tell the difference between a pointer to a character and a pointer to a character string — they are, in fact, the same. When `cout` is fed a

cout interprets char * differently than other pointers

(pointer to a) character string, it chooses to do the thing it is most likely being asked to do, namely, it displays the string. Thus the C++ code

```
long  l  = 0x41424344, // ASCII ABCD, left to right
     *lp = &l;
char *cp = (char *)lp;

cout << cp << " " << lp << endl;
```

produces the output

```
DCBA 0x8d710ffc
```

Thus a `char *` pointer always displays a character string and any other pointer type always displays its hex value. Some machines, depending on their internal architecture, might display the characters in the order 'ABCD'.

To get the actual location in memory pointed to by a `char` pointer, we would need to code something like

```
cout << (void *) cp << endl;
```

When we use `cin` to read into a character array (or a string pointed to by a `char *` pointer), `cin` behaves just as `scanf` does: it reads and stores characters up to the first blank, tab, or end of line. Thus the code

```
char s[100];
...
cin >> s;
```

cin separates words

given the input

nothing but words

would assign to s the character string "nothing".

One final word. Some C++s *buffer* stream output to the screen, that is, cout collects output until either an `endl` or a `cin` occurs. This is to improve performance. In rare circumstances where this is a problem, one can use the special cout stream manipulator **flush**, which forces everything collected so far to be displayed on the screen. To demonstrate the occurrence of buffering and the use of flush, consider the following situation: Programs often want to give some visual indication on the screen that they are working. One method, which we show below, is to output a period from time to time. We use a large do-nothing loop to simulate a lengthy process.

use flush to force output to screen

```
// pause.cpp -- test to see if cout buffers output
//  if the first line of output has different timing
//  from the second, buffering is occurring

#include <iostream.h>
```

```
#define PAUSELEN 500000L // suitable for 33Mhz 486 or VAX

void main( void )
{
   int i; long j;

   for ( i = 1; i <= 10; ++i ) { // line without flushing
       cout << '.';
       for ( j = 1; j <= PAUSELEN; ++j ) ; // wait
       }
   cout << endl;

   for ( i = 1; i <= 10; ++i ) { // same but with flushing
       cout << '.' << flush ;
       for ( j = 1; j <= PAUSELEN; ++j ) ; //wait
       }
   cout << endl;
}
```

If the program waits a long time to give the first line of output, then gives all the dots in quick succession, while the second line has short pauses between each dot, then buffering is in use. If both lines come out with the same timing, buffering is not in use. According to the author's experiments, GNU and Visual C++ buffer cout and Borland C++ doesn't. It never hurts to add the flush manipulators, except perhaps for a slight speed penalty. Note that flush isn't needed in baseout.cpp, above. The only place in this book that it will actually be *necessary* is in the example in Chapter 6.

cerr is used for error output

Another solution to the buffering problem is to use the cerr standard stream, which works exactly like cout except that it is never buffered and normal redirection doesn't send it away from the user's screen.

Exercises 1.2

1. Suppose that x, y, and z are int variables with values 19, 12, and 43, respectively. What is displayed by the following cout statements?

```
cout << "x = " << x << endl;
cout << x << " is between " << y << " and " << z << "." << endl;
cout << "The average of " << x << " and y is << " (x + y)/2
        << endl;
cout << oct << x << " " << y << " " << z << endl;
cout << hex << x << " " << y << " " << dec << z << endl
```

2. What (decimal) values are given to the int variables x, y, and z by the statement

```
cin >> x >> y >> z;
```

assuming each of the following lines of input:

```
24 -255 76
  23 023 0xA
```

```
-24 54 5.4                (make an educated guess here, then try it)
```

3.   What would you expect the following statement to do if it worked?

```
cin >> x >> y >> endl >> z;   // DOES NOT COMPILE!
```

4.   Suppose that x, y, and z are int variables with values 23, 14, and –5, respectively. Give cout statements to produce the following lines of output, with the number values coming from the variables:

```
The sum of 23, 14, and -5 is 32.
The hex value of 23 is 17.
23 > 14 > -5
14 = 016 = 0xE
```

(Note that if these are all in the same program, a dec indicator is needed somewhere.)

5.   Suppose that i is an int variable and c is a char variable. What is the output from the following code?

```
i = 'a';    // decimal value = 97
c = 97;
cout << "i = " << i << ", i + 1 = " << i + 1;
cout << "; c = " << c << ", c + 1 = " << c + 1 << endl;
cout << "With type casting, i + 1 = " << (char)(i + 1);
cout << " and c + 1 = " << (char)(c + 1) << endl;
```

6.   Suppose that x, y, and z are float variables with values 0.0091, 3.545000, and –67684.3, respectively. What is the output of the following code?

```
cout << x << " + " << y << " = " << x + y << "." << endl;
cout << "z * 100,000 = " << z * 1e5 << endl;
cout << "x * 1000 = " << x * 1000 << " and " <<
        "x / 100,000 " = x / 1e5 << endl;
```

7.   What would the output of the program baseout.cpp be if the input line were

123 123456 3.1415926535 3.1415926535

(Note: no '#' character. Recall that cin skips to the next non-blank character for input.)

8.   Write a function char *space(int n) which returns a pointer to a character string consisting of (up to 20) spaces. Thus the code

```
cout << "12345678901234567890" << endl;
cout << 42 << space(8) << 36 << endl;
```

would produce the output

```
12345678901234567890
42          36
```

9. a)   Some C and C++ compilers, for reasons of efficiency in the particular computer they are designed for, always assign character variables to an even address, or even an address divisible by 4, if they can. Test your compiler for this property by declaring

```
char c1, c2;
```

and using `cout` to display the addresses of `c1` and `c2`. (Note: you could conceivably get different results depending on whether the variables are local or global!)

b)   C and C++ compilers store local variables on a *stack*, whose structure need not concern you. In the following code

```
char *p1;

void f2( void )
{
    char c2;
    ...
}

void f1( void )
{
    char c1;

    p1 = & c1;
    f2();
}

void main( void )
{
    f1();
}
```

the `main` program calls `f1`, which calls `f2`. `f2` has access to both the address of `c1` (through `p1`) and `c2`. They are separated in memory by the amount of stack space used for `f1` to call `f2`. Find out how much that is. (Note that it may contain a little extra space for `c1` because of part a) above.) (Remarks on the program: (1) I didn't pass the address of `c1` as a parameter since then the distance between `c1` and `c2` would also contain the space necessary to pass the parameter. (2) I didn't put `c1` in `main` because some C compilers may put main program locals in global memory rather than in the stack.)

2. Reference Types

The reference type in C++ is a feature which in elementary applications adds greatly to the safety of C++ programs and in more advanced usage adds greatly to the power of the language. A **reference type** is a sort of constant, automatic pointer.

The following example will give something of the flavor of variables of reference type. Suppose that we declare

```
int a;
int &ra = a;  // ra permanently refers to a
```

Then use of a or ra within a program is interchangeable — they will always have the same value.

```
a = 14;    // also sets ra = 14
ra = -425; // also sets a = -425
```

In this situation &ra, the address of ra, would be the same as &a. Compare this to a similar treatment using pointers:

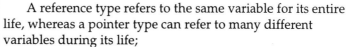

```
int a;
int *pa = &a; // pa points to a until it is changed
    ...
a = 14;       // also sets *pa = 14, if pa still points to a!!!
*pa = -425;   // also sets a = -425 (same caveat)
```

reference and pointer types compared

Note the difference between using pointers and reference types:

> A reference type refers to the same variable for its entire life, whereas a pointer type can refer to many different variables during its life;
>
> When a pointer is set (e.g. pa = &a) the address-of operator '&' must be used explicitly, whereas when a reference type is initialized '&' must *not* be used;
>
> When the value pointed to by a pointer is set or used, the '*' operator must be used, whereas with reference types, the '*' is not needed and must *not* be used.

most important use of reference types is for parameters

The examples above use 'ordinary variables', and I can see no legitimate use for reference types with such variables. On the other hand, reference types are extremely useful in function parameters and occasionally as a function return type. The following tables compare these three kinds of uses. For simplicity all the references will be to ints, but 'int' can be replaced by any C++ type. The 'ordinary variable' case will be shown shaded to remind you of its dubious utility.

11

Declaration of `int` Reference Type		
Ordinary Variable	Function Parameter	Function Return
`int &x = lvalue;`	`type Fun(...int &x...)`	`int &x( ... )`

There are two ways in which a reference type is assigned a value. When it is originally *created*, it is assigned an lvalue of the same type (here `int`) to reference. (An **lvalue** is anything that can appear on the left side of an assignment statement.) Once a variable of reference type has been created, it (and hence the lvalue it refers to) can be assigned any value of the correct type (here `int`). In what follows we will assume we have declared

```
int a, b[10]; // standard declarations for use with tables below
```

Creating References with an `int` Reference Type		
Ordinary Variable	Function Parameter	Function Return

`int &x = a,`
`    &y = b[3];`
	`type Fun( int &x,`
	`             int  &y  )`
	`{`
	`   ...`
	`}`
	`   ...Fun(   a,    b[3]`
	`)...`
		`int &x( ... ) {`
		`   ...`
		`   return a;`
		`}`
		`int &y( ... ) {`
		`   ...`
		`   return b[3];`
		`}`

Function parameters are created and initialized when the function is called, and cease to exist when the function is returned from. A function return reference type is created and initialized when the `return` statement is executed and destroyed when evaluation of the function call is finished. (Thus, function return types have an extremely short existence.)

To set a to 14 and b[3] to –257 in each case, we would code

Assigning Values to a and b[3]		
Ordinary Variable	Function Parameter	Function Return

`int & x = a,`
`    & y = b[3];`
`...`
`x = 14;`
`y = -257;`
	`type Fun( int & x,`
	`             int & y )`
	`{`
	`   x = 14;`
	`   y = -257;`
	`}`
	`   ...Fun(   a,   b[3]`
	`)...`
		`int & x( ... ) {`
		`   ...`
		`   return a;`
		`}`
		`int & y( ... ) {`
		`   ...`
		`   return b[3];`
		`}`
		`   ...`
		`x( ... ) = 14;`
		`y( ... ) = -257;`

Note the following *illegal* ways of creating reference type variables:

ILLEGAL Creation of Reference Types		
Ordinary Variable	Function Parameter	Function Return

`float r;`
`int & x = `**`14`**`,`
`    & y = `**`&14`**`;`
`    & z = `**`a + 1`**`;`
`    & w = `**`r`**`;`
	`type Fun( int & x,`
	`              int & y )`
	`{`
	`    ...`
	`}`
	`    ...Fun(   14,    &14`
	`)...`
		`int & x( ... ) {`
		`    ...`
		`    return 14;`
		`}`
		`int & y( ... ) {`
		`    ...`
		`    return &14;`
		`}`

14, &14, and a + 1 are illegal because they aren't lvalues, i.e., they cannot be used on the left side of an assignment statement, and r is illegal because it isn't a variable of the correct type. (But see 'A Cautionary Tale' in the Preface and Exercise 2–3 below.)

Let's give some useful examples involving reference parameters and function return types.

Example 2.1: Write a program Swap(x, y) which swaps the values of its two integer arguments. The following program fails, because C and C++ normally pass parameters *by value*; that is, the value of the parameter is passed *to* the function, but any changes to that value are *not* passed back to the caller.

```
// Incorrect version of Swap

void Swap( int x, int y)
{
   int temp = x;
   x = y;
   y = temp;   // exchanges x and y within Swap, but doesn't
               // affect a and b
}
   ...
   Swap( a, b );
```

Note that the function call Swap(14, 24) would be legal here, and we certainly wouldn't expect it to swap the values of two *constants*! The following program works,

```
// Traditional C version of Swap

void Swap( int *px, int *py)
{
   int temp = *px;
   *px = *py;
   *py = temp;   // exchanges a and b as well as *px and *py
}
   ...
   Swap( &a, &b );
```

but the C++ version is simpler and much safer:

```
// Swap using reference parameters

void Swap( int &x, int &y)
{
   int temp = x;
   x = y;
   y = temp;   // exchanges a and b
}
   ...
   Swap( a, b );
```

The method of passing parameters using reference types is exactly equivalent to Pascal **var** parameters and Ada **inout** parameters. Though use of parameters with reference types is safer and easier than passing pointers and dereferencing them manually, in fact the same code is generated in either method.

To show that a procedure such as Swap can be useful, consider the following:

Example 2.2: Write a function SelectionSort(A, n) to sort an array A of n integers using the selection sort. The selection sort works as follows:

```
for ( i = 0; i < n - 1; ++i ) {    // sorting A[0..n-1]
   let smallj be the index of the smallest element
      among A[i], ..., A[n - 1];
   Swap( A[i], A[smallj] );
   }
```

The function works because at the beginning of each iteration of the loop, we are assuming that A[0], ..., A[i - 1] are the smallest items in the array and are already sorted. The work of the loop is to allow us to add 1 to i and maintain that condition. The code is

```
// selsort.cpp -- selection sort

int &Swap( int &a, int &b )
   ...

void SelectionSort(int A[], int n)
{
   int i, j, smallj;

   --n; // n is 1 more than the top subscript
   for ( i = 0; i < n; ++i ) {
      for ( smallj = i, j = i + 1; j <= n; ++j )
         if ( A[j] < A[smallj] ) smallj = j;
      Swap( A[i], A[smallj] );
      }
}

void main ...
```

Note that we can pass parameters like A[i] with variable subscripts to reference parameters. However, if i = 22, the reference is fixed to A[22] on entry to the function, and the parameter continues to refer to A[22] even if i is changed in the function. Thus

```
int    i = 1,
       A[2] = { -18, 45 };

void aFun( int &x )
{
   cout << x << " ";
   i = 0;   // changes A[i] BUT NOT x!
   cout << x << endl;
}
   ...
   aFun( A[i] )
```

produces the output

```
45 45
```

Also, C++ declarations can occur anywhere, not just at the beginning of a { } block. I think this is a poor idea in general, but one place where it might be justified is in the declaration of the index for a `for` loop. For instance, the `SelectionSort` code could be replaced by

declarations can go anywhere in blocks

```
void SelectionSort(int A[], int n)
{
   for ( int i = 0; i < n; ++i ) {
      for ( int smallj = i, j = i + 1; j <= n; ++j )
         if ( A[j] < A[smallj] ) smallj = j;
      Swap( A[i], A[smallj] );
      }
}
```

The first `for` statement declares i and the second declares smallj and j. Such variables, once declared, become available throughout the remainder of the block, not just in the `for` loop. Thus if the following two statements are in a single block, the second is erroneous:

```
for (int i = ...
   ...
for (int i = ...   // ILLEGAL multiple declaration of i
```

Note though that smallj is available only within the block that is the body of the `for` i loop.

Now let us turn to reference return types for functions. It is harder to make a convincing case for these now, so I will give an unconvincing one. Returning large objects by reference saves copying, and for 'file objects' such as cout, a reference return is essential since a copy isn't the same thing.

Example 2.3: We are going to construct a function `Bigger( a, b )` which returns a *reference* to the larger of its arguments. Thus not only will we be able to use the larger value, as in `x = Bigger( a, b )`, we will also be able to *alter* the variable with the larger value *without knowing which one it is*! Thus `++Bigger( a, b )` will add 1 to whichever variable is larger. (I told you the example wasn't particularly compelling.) The function itself is easy to write:

```
int & Bigger( int & x, int & y )
{
   if ( x > y ) return x;
   else return y;
}
```

(Note that we could also replace the body of the function with `return ( x > y ) ? x : y;`) Then if we code

```
int a = 14, b = 25, x;
   ...
   x = Bigger( a, b );    // sets x = 25
   ++ Bigger( a, b ); // sets b = 26
```

Note that if we defined `Bigger` as follows

```
int & Bigger( int x, int y )  // Does not work properly!!
{ //     no &s:   ^        ^
   if ( x > y ) return x;
   else return y;
}
```

The reason that this version of `Bigger` doesn't work properly is that it returns a reference to one of the *local variables* x or y. By the time the outside world comes to use that fact, the function has been exited and the parameters, which are local to `Bigger`, no longer exist. `x = Bigger( a, b )` will probably work for the second version, but it isn't guaranteed to. `++Bigger( a, b )` on the other hand changes something which no longer exists, rather than a or b. I haven't found a C++ that indicates that there is a problem here. (See Exercise 2–4 below.)

Exercises 2

1. Suppose that we have declared

```
int    i = 5,     j = -27,
    *pi = &i, &ri = i;
```

What is the output from the following sequences of instructions?

```
cout << "*pi = " << *pi << "; ri = " << ri << endl;
i = 144;
cout << "*pi = " << *pi << "; ri = " << ri << endl;
pi = &j; ri = j;
cout << "*pi = " << *pi << "; ri = " << ri << endl;
```

```
i = 22;
cout << "*pi = " << *pi << "; ri = " << ri << endl;
j = 123;
cout << "*pi = " << *pi << "; ri = " << ri << endl;
```

2. What is printed by the following program?

```
#include <iostream.h>

void aFun( int a, int *pb, int &c )
{
    cout << "a = " << a << ", b = " << *pb << ", and c = "
            << c << endl;
    a = 11;  *pb = 22;  c = 33;
    cout << "a = " << a << ", b = " << *pb << ", and c = "
            << c << endl;
}

void main( void )
{
    int xa = 1001, xb = 2002, xc = 3003;

    cout << "xa = " << xa << ", xb = " << xb << ", and xc = "
            << xc << endl;
    aFun(xa, &xb, xc);
    cout << "xa = " << xa << ", xb = " << xb << ", and xc = "
            << xc << endl;
    xa = 1111, xb = 2222, xc = 3333;
    aFun(xa, &xb, xb );
    cout << "xa = " << xa << ", xb = " << xb << ", and xc = "
            << xc << endl;
}
```

3. Suppose that the following prototype declarations

```
void aFun( int &x );
void bFun( int *px );
```

have been given and i is an integer variable and j is an unsigned (integer) variable. Which of the following invocations of aFun are legal and which are illegal?

```
aFun(i);      aFun(&i);    aFun(i + 1);  aFun(33);  aFun(j);
bFun(i);      bFun(&i);    bFun(&i + 1);  bFun(33);  bFun(&(i + 1));
```

(**Note:** You should verify your answers with your C++ compiler. The answers vary slightly from compiler to compiler, and in the author's opinion, some which should be illegal aren't. See also 'A Cautionary Tale' in the Preface.)

4. Test your C++ compiler to see whether it gives errors for the following functions:

```
int &Bad1( int x )              int &Bad2( )
{                               {
   return x;                       int y;
}                                  return y;
                                }
```

(And see the note at the end of Exercise 3.)

5. What is the output from the following program?

```
#include <iostream.h>

char *pp = "positive",
     *pn = "negative";

void aFun( char * & p, int n )
{
   if (n < 0) p = pn;
   else p = pp;
}

void main( void )
{
   char *q = "neither";

   aFun( q, 3 );
   cout << q << endl;
   aFun( q, -17 );
   cout << q << endl;
}
```

6. Write a C++ function void cycle(index, limit) which causes index to run successively through the values 0, 1, ... limit-1, 0, 1, ... etc. Thus we have the following values for index before and after the call cycle(index, 1000);

index before	index after
0	1
1	2
...	
998	999
999	0

7. Suppose we declared int A[100], i = 22; and that A[i] = -456 for i = 0, ... 99. What values are changed, to what values, by Swap(A[i], i)? Same question for Swap(i, A[i]). (Reference parameter version of Swap.)

3. Extensions to Functions

In this section we will discuss three extremely useful C++ extensions of C related to functions. They are inline functions, default parameters, and overloaded functions. In particular, the ability to overload functions is one of the most powerful in the C++ language, and we will be occupied with it in one form or another for the rest of the book.

3.1 Inline Functions

Often it would be nice to encapsulate small pieces of code as functions. The problem is that passing parameters, calling a function, and returning from the call in a small function can take more space and time than the function code itself. In C, the `#define` statement is the only solution. For instance, the following code

dangers of #defines with parameters

```
#define MAX( x, y ) (x > y) ? x : y
```

causes the actual code `(a > b) ? a : b` to be substituted for `MAX( a, b )` wherever it occurs in the program, and there is no overhead from call, return, and parameter passing. One must be careful with such code, though. The code `MAX( a++, b++ )` or `MAX( a, b ) + 1` would probably have unintended results.[1] Another common problem is demonstrated by

```
#define PROD( x, y ) x * y    // poor #define
```

If the user entered `PROD( a+b, c+d )` the result would be `a + b*c + d` rather than `(a+b) * (c+d)` as was probably intended. C programmers must learn to enclose parameters in parentheses automatically:

```
#define PROD( x, y ) (x) * (y) // better #define
```

C++ allows one to define ordinary functions (presumably small ones) with the 'storage type' **inline**. C++ then makes an effort to copy the code into each place where the function is called. This cuts down on execution time, at the expense of having multiple copies of the function in your program. The two functions above could be written

inline functions are real functions that (usually) compile like #defines

```
inline int MAX( int x, int y ) { return (x > y) ? x : y; }

inline int PROD( int x, int y ) { return x * y; }
```

---

[1] `MAX( a++, b++ )` would cause either a or b to be incremented twice (and the final value is implementation dependent, depending on when the incrementation takes place). Because '+' has higher precedence than '?:', `(a > b) ? a : b + 1` compiles as `(a > b) ? a : (b + 1)` rather than `((a > b) ? a : b) + 1`.

Note that when you declare a function `inline` you must give the function body on the spot. If you didn't, you'd be saying to the compiler, 'include the code for this procedure wherever it is called, but I'm not going to tell you what the code is.'

When functions are declared `inline`, you must declare parameter types and a function value type. This is both an advantage and a disadvantage. On the plus side, it makes for safer programming but on the minus side, our `#defined` versions of MAX and PROD work for any numeric type as parameters. (As we will see in section 3.3, it is possible to get the effect of multiple parameter types by overloading inline functions, but it's more work.)

Functions declared `inline` can also use local variables:

```
inline void SWAP( int &x, int &y )
{
    int temp = x;
    x = y;
    y = temp;
}
```

The specification of a function as `inline` is only a *suggestion* to the compiler. If the function is long it is unlikely to be compiled inline and if it is recursive, it can't be.

Exercises 3.1

1. Define `inline` functions for the following:

```
int sgn( double x )    // returns 0 if x = 0, -1 if x < 0,
          //  1 if x > 0
double pos( double x ) // returns x if x >= 0, 0 if x < 0
```

2. a) Define an `inline` function `int  imul3( int  x )` which returns `3 * x` by computing `(x << 1) + x`.

   b) Suppose we had defined the following function:

```
#define dmul3( x )  ((x << 1) + x)
```

If `i` is an `int` variable with value 3, what is the value of `dmul3( i + 1 )`? of `dmul3( i << 1 )`? (Hint: one of them works and one doesn't.)

   c) Redefine `dmul3` correctly as follows:

```
#define dmul3( x )  (((x) << 1) + (x))
```

   i) What is the effect of evaluating `dmul3(a + 3 * b/(1 + i))`, as opposed to doing the same thing with `imul3`?

   ii) What about evaluating `dmul3( i++ )` as opposed to doing it with `imul3`?

iii) What if D is a `double` variable with value 3.5 and we try to evaluate `dmul3( D )`, as opposed to evaluating `imul3( D )`?

(You may well have to determine some of these results by experimentation, which is part of the point of these exercises.)

3.2 Default Parameters

C++ allows **default** values to be specified for function parameters. The default value is used for the parameter when no value is given for it in a function call.

For instance, we can write

```
void printMe( int x = 3 )      // x is given the value 3 if
                               // no parameter is specified
{ cout << x << endl; }
   ...
   printMe( 45 );              // displays 45
   printMe( );                 // displays the default value 3
```

Usually functions are first **declared** in a prototype and then **defined**, that is, their actual code given, later on. Parameter defaults should be declared only once, in the prototype. For example,

```
void printMe( int x = 3 ); // declaration (note ';')
                           // x has default value of 3
   ...
   printMe( 45 );          // displays 45
   printMe( );             // displays the default value 3
   ...
void printMe( int x )      // definition (no ';')
                           //Default must not be respecified.
{ ...
```

In a function with multiple parameters, once one parameter has been given a default value all the parameters that follow must also be given default values. For example, if we have declared

```
void aFun( int x, int y = 5, float z = 18.2 );
```

then the call `aFun(1, 2)` is equivalent to the call `aFun(1, 2, 18.2)` and the call `aFun(1)` is equivalent to the call `aFun(1, 5, 18.2)`. The call `aFun( )` would be illegal (x has no default value). Also, the declaration

```
void bFun( int x, int y = 5, float z );    // ILLEGAL
```

would be illegal. (Calling such a function without a second parameter would require two consecutive commas, which was deemed error-prone.) Expressions may be used in default values:

```
int x = 1;
void cFun( int d = 3 * x + 1);
```

```
x = 15;
cFun( );    // equivalent to the call cFun(46)
```

A variable used in the default expression may have two definitions, one in force at the time the function is *declared* and another where it is *executed*. The variables in force at the time of the declaration of the default value are used to evaluate it, not those at the time the function is called. Thus in the following example, the declaration int x = 15 is used rather than int x = 2 in the call to dFun.

```
int x = 15, y = 27;
void dFun( int e = x + y );     // always uses x and y above

void main( void )
{
    int x = 2;

    y = 300;
    dFun ( ); // equivalent to dFun( 315 )
```

The variables involved in default value expressions must all be global. Thus the following declaration is illegal:

```
void eFun( int x, int y = x ); // ILLEGAL
```

Exercises 3.2

1. Suppose that we have declared the following function:

```
void aFun( int a, int b = 14, int c = -24 );
    ...
void aFun( int a, int b, int c );
{
    cout << a << " " << b << " " << c << endl;
}
```

What is displayed by the following code?

```
aFun( 3, 5, 7 );
aFun( 3, 5 );
aFun( 3 );
```

2. Write a prototype for the function space from Exercise 1.2–8, which causes the call space() to return a pointer to a string consisting of one space character.

3. Write a prototype and function definition for a function void inc(int &x, int n) which increments x by n. When the second parameter is missing, increment x by 1.

4. Write a prototype and function definition for the function `float distance(
float x1, float y1, float x2, float y2)` which returns the distance
between the points (x1, y1) and (x2, y2) in two-dimensional space. The distance
between these two points is

$$\sqrt{(x1-x2)^2+(y1-y2)^2}$$

The C square root function is `sqrt` (prototype in `math.h`). Arrange it so that if
your function is called with only two parameters, representing one point, the
function returns the distance to the point (0, 0).

5. Write a prototype and definition for a function `void persist( int n )`
which has the property that the call `persist()` uses n equal to its last value + 1.
(Initially assume a last value of 0.) The body of `persist` might do anything, but
for the purposes of this problem, just have it write out n on a line by itself. Then

```
persist( 347 );       // displays 347
persist( )            // displays 348
persist( 18 );        // displays 18
persist( );           // displays 19
persist( );           // displays 20
```

(Hint: define a global, or even better, a *static* local, variable `lastn`.)

3.3 Function Overloading

A function name with more than one declaration is said to be an **overloaded
function**. Each declaration of the name must have a different number of parameters
and/or different types of parameters so that C++ can determine from the function
call which version of the function to apply. (The type the function returns cannot
be used to distinguish names.) C++ determines which version of the function to
use by picking the one that most closely matches the actual function invocation in
type and number of parameters. Consider the following examples:

```
void aFun( int x )          { /* definition 1 */ }
void aFun( int x, int y )   { /* definition 2 */ }
void aFun( double x )       { /* definition 3 */ }

    aFun( 3 );      // calls definition 1
    aFun( 3.5 )     // calls definition 3
    aFun( 1, 2 )    // calls definition 2
```

It would have been an error to give y a default value in definition 2 because the call
`aFun(3)` would not have been able to distinguish between definitions 1 and 2.

If there isn't an exact match, C++ has a very complicated scheme for
determining how actual parameter types are cast to make the function choice. The
complete set of rules, with examples, occupies twenty-two pages in Ellis and

*overloading can
be hazardous to
your (mental)
health*

Stroustrup (§§ 13–13.2; see the References). A simple example of the surprises that can occur is

```
void ofun( int x );
void ofun( float x );
   ...
   ofun( 3.5 );
```

C++ refuses to compile this program because numbers with decimal points in expressions (here, '3.5') are assumed to be of type `double`, and C++ can't decide whether to convert 3.5 to `float` or `int`! The program was rewritten with an additional `ofun` with `double` parameter, with each `ofun` defined as follows:

```
void ofun( myType x )
{
   cout << "ofun called with myType parameter" << endl;
}
```

With a main program of

```
void main( void )
{
   ofun( 3 );
   ofun( 3.5 );
   ofun( (float)3.5 );
}
```

I got the output

```
ofun called with int parameter
ofun called with double parameter
ofun called with float parameter
```

My advice is not to try to figure out complicated type casts when using overloaded functions. I think it extremely confusing and error prone. Instead,

RULE 19

> To avoid problems with overloaded functions, either
>   i)   Include one version of the function for all possible combinations of parameter types,
>   ii)   Explicitly cast all variables that don't match parameter types, or
>   iii)   Add debugging messages to each version of the function so you can see which version is being called.

Method i) can be implemented efficiently by making the 'unnecessary' declarations `inline` functions. For instance, in the original example above, we could have declared

```
inline void ofun( double x ) { ofun( (float)x ); }
```

The problem with both methods i) and ii) is that they require anticipating that there might be a problem, which may not be so easy. For method iii), we could for instance use the standard C technique on the "ofun called..." messages:

```
void ofun( type x )
{
#ifdef DEBUG
   cout << "ofun called with type parameter" << endl;
#endif
   ...
```

Overloaded functions can be used as a substitute for default parameters. For instance, the declaration of aFun in section 3.2

```
void aFun( int x, int y = 5, float z = -18.2 );
```

could be rewritten

```
void aFun( int x, int y, float z );
inline void aFun( int x, int y )     { aFun( x, y, -18.2 ); }
inline void aFun( int x )     { aFun( x, 5, -18.2 ); }
```

Exercises 3.3

default parameters preferable to overloading

1. a) Consider the following overloaded function definition:

```
int sum( int a, int b )
{
   return a + b;
}

int sum( int a, int b, int c )
{
   return a + b + c;
}

int sum( int a, int b, int c, int d )
{
   return a + b + c + d;
}
```

Rewrite the sum function as a single function with default parameter values. Why is the rewritten version preferable to the version given above?

overloading preferable to default parameters

b) Consider the following function with a default parameter:

```
int theSum, theCount;

void sum( int a = -999 )
{
   if ( a == -999 )
      theSum = theCount = 0;
```

```
        else {
            theSum += a;
            ++ theCount;
        }
    }
```

Rewrite this function as two separate overloaded functions. Why is the rewritten version preferable to the version given above?

overloading strlen   2.   a)   Write an overloaded version of the `strlen` function that takes an *integer* argument and returns the number of characters required to display the integer. Don't actually compute the character string — look at the various ranges of the argument. For instance, if the parameter is between 0 and 9 (inclusive), the value of the function is 1.

overloading abs   b)   Some authors of mathematical treatments of strings use $|s|$, the usual notation for absolute value, to represent the length of a string *s*. Write an overloaded version of the `abs` function so that `abs ( s )` = `strlen( s )` when s is a `char *` variable.

3.   a)   Write an overloaded function `char *MyType( type x )` (in several versions) which returns the type of its argument x in the form `"char"`, `"int"`, `"float"`, or `"double"`.

b)   Assume you have declared `char c = 'a'; char i = 5;` use `MyType` to determine the data type of `c + 1` and `i + 1.0`.

4.   Contrary to some textbooks, C++ will use the types and number of the *arguments* to a function to determine which overloaded version of the function to use, but will *not* use the type of the *value* of the function in this determination.

a)   Show that C++ will not allow you to declare two functions with the same name and arguments but different return types.

b)   Show that C++ will allow you to declare two functions with the same name but different argument *and* return types, but will choose the particular function based *solely* on argument types.

4. Memory Allocation and Release

C++ has a type-safe way of allocating and freeing memory using the operators `new` and `delete` (which are reserved words in C++). For any C++ data type *myType*,

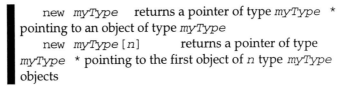

> new *myType*   returns a pointer of type *myType* `*`
> pointing to an object of type *myType*
>   new *myType* [n]   returns a pointer of type
> *myType* `*` pointing to the first object of n type *myType*
> objects

If we have declared

```
myType *p, *pa;
```

then the C++ statements

use new instead of malloc

```
p = new myType;
pa = new myType[20];
```

are equivalent to the C statements

```
p = (myType *)malloc( sizeof(myType) );
pa = (myType *)malloc( 20 * sizeof(myType) );
```

As usual, `p` and/or `pa` will be set to the null pointer if the allocation cannot be performed.

New is generally safer than `malloc` because `malloc` returns a `void *` pointer, which can point to anything and whose value can be stored in any pointer type. Thus no type checking is done. In addition, if *myType* is a *class* (to be defined in Chapter 5), `new` causes any special initialization for the class to be performed, whereas `malloc` doesn't. In case an *array* of class objects is allocated using `new`, as in new *myType* [20] above, *every item in the array is initialized* in this way.

There are no corresponding replacements for `calloc` and `realloc`, though the fact (mentioned above) that `new` automatically initializes classes can be used for more powerful purposes than `calloc` .

As one often wishes to allocate storage for `struct`s, unions, and enums, a difference from C should be noted. In C, a `struct`, union, or enum data type name must be used in company with the defining keyword (`struct`, union, or enum). In C++, the appropriate keyword need not be mentioned. Thus consider declarations:

```
struct s { ... };
union u { ... };
enum e { ... }

s x1; u y1; e z1;      // ILLEGAL in C, legal in C++
```

27

```
struct s x2; union u y2; enum e z2    // allowed in both C and C++
```

and expressions in C++

```
... new s ... // = new struct s, returns s*( = struct s*) type
... new u ... // = new union u, returns u*( = union u*) type
... new e ... // = new enum e, returns e*( = enum e*) type
```

use delete
instead of free

Memory allocated with new should be freed with the delete operation. To free the memory allocated above, use

```
delete p;          // for single objects allocated by new
delete [] pa;      // for arrays allocated by new
```

Delete should be used only on pointers set by the new operation. Thus code like

```
myType *p, *q, r;
    ...
p = new myType[100];
q = &r;
++ p;          // now points to (original p)[1]
    ...
delete p;   // likely to be disastrous
delete q;   // likely to be disastrous
```

probably won't work. Delete applied to the null pointer is guaranteed to work properly (i.e., to do nothing).

New and delete should always be used with classes (to be defined in Chapter 5) as they guarantee that special constructor and destructor functions are invoked. You should not use free with new or delete with malloc.

Exercises 4

1. Suppose that we have made the following declarations:

```
char *p;
int *q;
double *r;
struct s { int a, b; } *t;
```

Replace the following C-style statements with C++ ones:

```
p = (char *)malloc( 24 );
q = (int *)malloc( sizeof( int ) );
r = (double *)malloc( 200 * sizeof( double );
s = (struct s *)malloc( sizeof( struct s ));
    ...
free( p );
free( q );
free( r );
free( s );
```

2.   Write code to set a char * variable s pointing to a memory area containing the contents of the char * variable s1 followed by the contents of the char * variable s2. That is, s is to be the concatenation of s1 followed by s2. Use new to allocate memory for s to point to.

5. Classes

The most important addition of C++ to C is the notion of the *class*. Classes are a powerful tool for implementing Object-Oriented Programs, which we will demonstrate in Chapters 6 and 10, and in giving concrete representations for abstract data types.

An **abstract data type** (ADT) is a description of the properties and operations of a class of objects without concern for implementation. For instance, the *stack* as an ADT is an ordered collection of items accessible at only one end (the *top*) via the abstract operations *push(x)* (add x to the top of the stack) and *pop()* (remove the item from the top of the stack and return its value). This description says nothing about how the stack ADT will be actually implemented — whether for instance as an array or as a linked list.

The traditional way to implement an ADT has been with a `struct` to contain the actual data values (in the case of the stack ADT, the `struct` contains the list of items on the stack and the 'top' indicator) and a collection of functions performing the operations.

In C++, an ADT is implemented as a **class**, which is much like a `struct` except that in addition to the *data* associated with the ADT, the class definition also contains the functions to perform all of the abstract operations on objects of the class.

As the class corresponds to a data *type*, it is used to declare actual *instances* of that type, which are called **class objects**. The functions of a class are held in common by all objects of that class, while each individual object has its own set of values for the data items. These data items can be protected so that only those functions in the class or 'blessed' by the class can operate on the class data. This mechanism can be used to ensure data integrity, i.e., that all data items in the class have values which are legal and coherent with the other values of the object. As an example, a 'date' class can guarantee that such dates as Feb. 29, 1967 cannot occur.

Classes and objects were first used in the discrete system simulation language Simula 67 developed at the Norwegian Computer Center. C++ classes are recognizably similar to Simula 67 classes. However C++ has added protection techniques and a lot of syntactic sugar (some of which we have already seen) which can make working with C++ classes more like working directly with the ADT than working with the nitty-gritty of the concrete implementation.

5.1 Some Basic Terminology

The general form of a **class declaration** is

```
class classname {
    declaration₁
    declaration₂
        . . .
    declarationₙ
```

```
};      // Note the terminating ';'. It's easy to forget.
```

where the *declaration*s can be any C-style data declaration, any function declaration *or complete definition*, and certain special function declarations. The data items of a class are called **data members** and the functions in the class are called **member functions**. Declarations of data and function members can be interspersed in any order.

In addition the class declaration can contain the labels `public:` and `private:` which give protection to members of the class to access from outside the class. Declarations following the **public** label are accessible to everyone, while

> Declarations following the **private** label can only be accessed by member functions in the class.

One can change back and forth between `public` and `private` at will.[2]

The specification of private data members is also an aid in **information hiding**, the attempt to make information available only to those parts of the program which need it. This is an attempt to localize program behavior so that changes in one part are less likely to have unsuspected effects on other parts — rather like watertight doors in ships which allow the effect of a leak to be localized.

In C++ terminology, a block of storage at program run-time representing a particular type of data is called an **object**. Thus if we declare

```
int a, *pi = new int;
```

then `pi` is a pointer object, and `a` and `*pi` are integer objects. If the data type is a class, *its* objects are called **class objects**. For instance, if the class `classname` is declared as above, the declaration

```
classname C, D, *pC;
```

declares C and D as class objects of `classname` and pC as a pointer to such a class object. (Notice that the keyword `class` is optional when declaring class objects.)

When a class object is created, C++ only needs to reserve memory for the *data* members of the class. A single copy of the function members is used in common by all objects of the class. When a member function of a particular object is called, C++ passes a hidden parameter represented by the keyword **this**, which is a pointer to the data member storage for the object.

inside member functions, 'this' points to the object that called the function

Reference to function and data members of a class object is reminiscent of the notation for `struct`s. Suppose we have declared

```
class aClass {
   ...
   int d;        // typical data member
   ...
   void f( aClass o )    // a member function, which has an aClass
```

_____

[2] An intermediate level of protection, `protected`, is introduced in section 9.2.

```
                              //  object as parameter
        ...
};

aClass   o1, o2,     // aClass objects
         *po = o1     // pointer to an aClass object, initially,
o1;
```

Then

> o1.d and po -> d   refer to o1's data
> member d
> o1.f(o2)   and   po->f(o2)   evaluate o1's version of
>   f() with parameter o2
>   When we evaluate o1.f(o2), this = &o1 and o =
> o2
>   During this evaluation, inside the definition of f(),
> this -> d is equivalent to d (= o1.d)
> this -> f(...) is equivalent to f(...) (= o1.f(...)
>)

Because of the last two statements,

RULE

> The keyword 'this' is usually only used to refer to the class
> object as a whole.

5.2 A Substantial Example

In this section we will construct an implementation of the ADT *Date*. A Date will record the month, day, and year. Initially there will be three operations defined on dates — addition or subtraction of an integer number (days) to a date giving another date and subtraction of two dates giving an integer number (days). The intuitive meaning of these operations should be clear from the following examples:

> "March 24, 1983" + 14 = "April 7, 1983"
> "January 3, 1954" – 25 = "December 9, 1953"
> "June 24, 1996" – "June 24, 1995" = 366

A class is generally *declared* in a file `classname.h` and the non-trivial member function *definitions* are given in a file `classname.cpp`. In the case of the Date class, we might have three files

```
// date.h--declarations for the Date class

class Date {
   declaration of data items and member functions for Date
};
```

```
// date.cpp--implementations of Date class operations

#include "date.h"
  member function definitions
```

```
// myprog.cpp--a user program which uses the Date class

#include "date.h"
  ...
Date birthday, anniversary, *pd;     // Date is now a data
type
  ...
  code to perform operations on dates
```

When we are developing classes for reuse, date.cpp would be compiled and perhaps kept in a library. In the link stage of constructing myprog, the compiled version of date.cpp would be combined with it.

As was mentioned in the last section, data and functions can be declared private to protect them. To simplify things though, we will start with everything public and add the protection later on.

There are a variety of ways we could represent a date, for instance as three integers representing month, day, and year or as the number of days since some fixed date. The first representation is more convenient when communicating with the real world and the second is more convenient when doing arithmetic with dates, so to avoid making a decision, we will use *both* representations simultaneously. For days before the fixed date, 'days since' will be negative, and if we wish to represent as many as 100 years, we may need a long int for it. Our first pass at the date.h file is

```
// date1.h--a first pass at the Date class

class Date {
    public:
        int month, day, year;
        long daysSince;      // Jan 1, BASEYEAR

        Date add( long n );
        Date sub( long n );
        long sub( Date d );
};
```

public data
members are
dangerous!
We will take care
of this later

The declarations of member functions above assume that the actual definitions will be given elsewhere.

If the *definition* of a member function is given inside the class declaration, the function is assumed to be *inline*.

If we declare

```
Date d1, d2; long n;
```

Then we can write operations on Dates as follows

```
d2 = d1.add( 3 );      // d2 = "d1 + 3"
d1 = d2.sub( 14 );     // d1 = "d2 - 14"
n = d1.sub( d2 );      // n = "d1 - d2"
```

Notice that the 'sub' member function is overloaded.

The '.add()' and '.sub()' notation is not very appealing, but C++ comes to our rescue by allowing us to use the more expressive '+' and '−' notation as on the right. We do this by declaring **operator functions** which **overload the + and − operations**:

```
Date operator + ( int n );

...
d2 = d1 + 3;
```

'd1 + 3' is actually short for the notation d1.operator+(3). Most C++ operators can be overloaded this way.[3] However,

> At least one of the operands of an overloaded operator must be a class object.

The revised form of date.h is

```
// date2.h--use of overloaded operators

class Date {
  public:
    int month, day, year;
    long daysSince;     // Jan 1, BASEYEAR

    Date operator + ( long n );
    Date operator - ( long n );
    long operator - ( Date d );
};
```

We can easily implement two of our operator functions inline. The new version of date.h is

```
// date3.h--implement member functions inline.

class Date {
  public:
    int month, day, year;
    long daysSince;     // Jan 1, BASEYEAR

    Date operator + ( long n )
```

---

[3]Included are new, delete, () (function evaluation), [] (subscripting), and unary operators such as *, !, and &. Excluded are ., ?:, and sizeof.

```
Date operator - ( long n ) { return *this + ( - n ); }
long operator - ( Date d )
   { return daysSince - d.daysSince; }
};
```

Note (1) the use of this as a pointer to the date on the left side of the subtraction operation, so that it can be passed to the + operator; (2) the use of daysSince unqualified, representing its value for the Date invoking the function, i.e., the Date on the left side of the subtraction; and (3) the use of d.daysSince to refer to the daysSince data member in another Date.

The keyword inline is not necessary for the two operator -'s because as we said before: functions defined within a class declaration are assumed to be inline.

Thus far we have avoided the messy question of how the Date member variables are initialized. Clearly it is very important that 'month, day, year' represent the same date as daysSince! One of the most powerful consequences of defining member functions within classes is that

RULE 9

‖ Classes can (and should) guarantee that their class objects
‖ always contain valid data.

The first way in which C++ helps us maintain the integrity of a class is that whenever a class object is created, C++ automatically initializes it using a special member function the programmer defines called a **constructor function**. The general form of the constructor function declaration is ClassName(initialization parameters).[4] By overloading the constructor function, we can create class objects in a variety of useful ways. For the Date class we will use three, which are declared as follows:

```
// Constructors:
Date( int m, int d, int y );    // init month, day, year
Date( long dS );                //        // init daysSince
Date( void );                   // init with today's date
```

The general form of the first Date constructor will be

```
...Date( int m, int d, int y )
{
   // verify that m, d, and y constitute a legal date
   ...
   month = m; day = d; year = y;
   // compute daysSince
}
```

---

[4]Actually the term *constructor* is a little misleading. When an object of a class is created, C++ *automatically* creates the storage for its data members. The constructor then fills the members with values and/or does anything else it wants.

The constructors are sufficiently complicated that they will be defined in the date.cpp file, to be discussed later.

Notice that

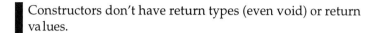

> Constructors don't have return types (even void) or return values.

This is perhaps because the main work of the constructor, allocating and returning storage for member data, is not explicitly stated.

Date(void) is called the **default constructor** as it can be called without arguments (or parentheses). Whenever a Date is declared with no parameters, this constructor is used.

RULE

> Always define a default constructor.

If you don't, C++ will define a *default* default constructor, which does nothing useful. (A constructor all of whose parameters have default values will act as the default constructor as it can be called with no parameters.)

We can now make declarations of Dates as follows:

```
Date  independence( 7, 4, 1776 ),
      today,  // uses default constructor
      birthday( 11, 19, 52 ), tomorrow = today + 1;
```

or create 'anonymous' Dates with pointers pointing to them:

```
Date *pd = new Date( 9, 21, 43 ), *qd;
   ...
   qd = new Date;      // defaults to today
```

The notation

```
Date independence = Date( 7, 4, 1776 ), today = Date();
```

can also be used and is in every way equivalent to the first way we initialized the variables independence and today. This second method, though, can be used to initialize *arrays* of Dates, as in

```
Date Birthday[] = { Date( 5, 1, 45), ... };
```

Expressions like Date(6, 6, 1944) can also be used in expressions, and serve as the 'constant' values of the Date data type.

A constructor can also be used to program operator+:

```
class Date {
      ...
    Date operator + ( long n )
       { return Date( daysSince + n ); }
      ...
```

```
};
```

We could also have written the code

```
// alternative form of operator+
    { Date d( daysSince + n ); return d; }
```

but the second version is less efficient since in it, C++ creates one `Date d` and then copies it into the return value of the function. The first version doesn't have to do that copy.

The second method of maintaining the integrity of data members is to make them private, so that only member functions can manipulate them directly. In fact I would suggest the following:

RULE 19

‖ All data members in a class should be private.

We give access to data members where appropriate using simple inline member functions that I call **accessers**. For example,

```
// sample accesser member function
int getMonth( void ) { return month; }
```

There is no loss of efficiency because the function is inline, and C++ generates the same code it would if you could access the data item directly.

We may also want to allow the user to set values of some data members, while of course maintaining the integrity of the object data. I call functions to do this **setters**. For instance, we might postulate a member function `void setDate( int m, int d, int y )` which could be used by a user of the `Date` class, as well as by the corresponding constructor function. Thus we can allow the user to change `Date`s without allowing him or her to set the month to 42.

Let's collect all our ideas so far.

```
// date.h--final (for now) version

class Date {
  private:
     int month, day, year;
     long daysSince;      // Jan 1, BASEYEAR
  public:
   // constructors
     Date( int m, int d, int y ) { setDate( m, d, y ); }
     Date( long dS ) { setDate( dS ); }
     Date( void ) { setDate( ); }    // defaults to today

   // accessers
     int getMonth( void ) { return month; }
     int getDay( void )   { return day; }
     int getYear( void )  { return year; }

   // setters
     void setDate( int m, int d, int y );
```

```
        void setDate( long dS );
        void setDate( void );

    // member functions
      Date operator + ( long n )
        { return Date( daysSince + n ); }
      Date operator - ( long n ) { return *this + ( - n ); }
      long operator - ( Date & d )
        { return daysSince - d.daysSince; } // see Note below
};
```

Note that even though daysSince is now private, it can still be accessed for other class objects in the same class *within a member function of the class*.

Note also that setDate doesn't have to be declared before it is used! This is because

> Any function body in a class can use all data and function members, *even those declared after it.*

This is an appropriate point to discuss another useful principle for writing functions which have class objects as parameters and/or return values.

RULE 9

> Class objects should *almost* always be passed to functions and returned as function values by *reference*.

For instance, Date objects would be passed and returned as Date &. This rule is certainly reasonable because class objects usually have a lot of storage devoted to data members, so it is more efficient to pass and return a pointer to the object. The functions operator+ and operator- above show one of the few situations when *returning by value is necessary*: We cannot return a reference in operator+ since the reference would be to Date(daysSince + n), which is a temporary object that disappears when the function containing it exits.

Passing objects by reference works even where perhaps it shouldn't. For instance, passing a 'constant' Date object of the form Date(7, 4, 1776) as a reference parameter to operator+ can be used in an expression like

```
long N = Date( 5, 14, 1994 ) - Date( 7, 4, 1776 ); // LEGAL!!
```

(See 'A Cautionary Tale' in the Preface.)

Finally, we will implement the remaining three member functions, the three setter functions in a .cpp file of the following form:

```
// date.cpp--implement member function of class Date

#include "date.h"

Date::setDate(int m, int d, int y)
{
   ...
}
```

```
Date::setDate( long dS )
{
    ...
}

Date::setDate( void ) // Today's date
{
    ...
}
```

The prefix `Date::` indicates that the function being defined is a member function of the `Date` class. ':: ' is called the **scope operator**.

Returning today's date is the easiest. We will use the UNIX functions `time` and `localtime`. The latter returns, among other things, the current month, day, and year. This function is also available in many non-UNIX C's and C++'s. The code for `Date()` is

```
#include <time.h>
    ...
Date::Date( void )
{
    time_t t;
    struct tm *pt;

    time( &t );                     // get mysterious t
    pt = localtime( &t );     // interpret mysterious t
    setDate( pt -> tm_mon + 1, pt -> tm_mday, pt -> tm_year );
}
```

The remaining two functions are rather complex and somewhat similar, so I'll only do the one that converts 'month, day, year' to 'daysSince'. The other is on the disk that comes with this book. Now we must finally choose BASEYEAR. I chose 1970 because that's what UNIX uses, and maybe that might someday come in handy.

We will deal with the possibility of an illegal date by using the C **assert** facility. Its general form is

```
#include <assert.h>
    ...
    assert ( condition );
```

If `condition` is false when the assert statement is executed, a message to that effect is displayed and execution terminated. Otherwise execution continues as before. To test and set a `Date` we will use the following:

```
#define BASEYEAR 1970 5
```

---

[5]C++ allows a more structured way to declare such constants, by putting the keyword `const` in front of any variable declaration, as in `const int BASEYEAR = 1970`. The main use of `const` is in declaring parameters to functions and thus

```
static monthDays[] = { 0 /* dummy */,
    31, 28, 31, 30, 31, 30, 31, 31, 30, 31, 30, 31 };

static int leapYear( int year )
{ return (year % 4) == 0 &&
            (year % 100 != 0 || year % 400 == 0); }
```

To make the calculations a little simpler, we will cheat a little and temporarily alter the length of February. The assertions are then simple:

```
#include <assert.h>
    ...
  monthDays[2] += leapYear( y );      // temporarily

  assert( m >= 1 && m <= 12 );
  assert( 1 <= d && d <= monthDays[m]);
  if ( y < 100 ) y += 1900;  // allows dates like Date( 2, 3, 94
)
```

We can start the conversion process by computing the number of days since Jan. 1 of the given year y:

```
daysSince = d - 1; // gets us to the first of month m
while ( --m ) daysSince += monthDays[m];
    // daysSince = number of days since Jan 1, y
monthDays[2] = 28; // NOW restore February
```

To account for the years, we have two possibilities depending on whether y is before or after 1970. We take care of this as follows:

```
while ( y >= BASEYEAR ) {
    daysSince += 365 + leapYear( --y );
    }
while ( y < BASEYEAR ) {
    daysSince -= 365 + leapYear( y++ );
    }
```

The beginning of date.cpp is now

```
// date.cpp--the implementations

#include "date.h"
#include <time.h>
#include <assert.h>
```

---

protecting them from change by the function. The rules for const parameters are messy and complex and in my opinion, not worth the trouble. The book *Windows++* by Paul DiLascia (see the Bibliography) develops 140 pages of sophisticated C++ code and uses const perhaps half a dozen times, all in trivial ways. Except for exercise 5.2–8 below, we won't use const in this book.

```
#define BASEYEAR 1970

static monthDays[] = { 0 /* dummy */,
      31, 28, 31, 30, 31, 30, 31, 31, 30, 31, 30, 31 };

static int leapYear( int year )
{  return (year % 4) == 0 &&
              (year % 100 != 0 || year % 400 == 0); }

void Date::setDate( int m, int d, int y )
{
   monthDays[2] += leapYear(y);                    //      temporary
expedient

   assert( m >= 1 && m <= 12 );
   assert( d >= 1 && d <= monthDays[m] );
   if ( y < 100 && y >= 0) y += 1900;

   month = m; // do the easy stuff
   day = d;
   year = y;

   daysSince = d - 1; // move to beginning of month m

   while ( --m )        // move to beginning of year y
      daysSince += monthDays[m];

   monthDays[2] = 28; // put it back like it belongs

   // now move year to Jan 1, BASEYEAR; only one of the
   // following loops will actually be executed

   while ( y >= BASEYEAR ) {
      daysSince += 365 + leapYear( --y );
      }
   while ( y < BASEYEAR ) {
      daysSince -= 365 + leapYear( y++ );
      }
}

void setDate( long dS )
{
   ...
```

We used different names for the parameters to setDate (m, d, and y) than we did for the data members we were initializing (month, day, and year). For instance, we used m as a parameter to initialize the month data member. This is because if we used

```
void Date::setDate( int month, ...
   ...
   month = m onth ;        // ERROR
```

the two occurrences of month in the assignment statement would both refer to the *parameter* month, and the data member month wouldn't get initialized! You could get around this by writing

```
this -> month = month;
```

but this kind of thing is easy to forget, and suggests another

 RULE

‖ Avoid using the same name for more than one variable.

Exercises 5.2

1. There can be only one default constructor in a class. Why?

2. Write a statement which adds 1 to the year of a Date d, and a second statement which adds 1 to the month of d. Why would it be dangerous to allow a user to do this by simply writing ++d.year or ++d.month? This exercise shows why it can be important not to allow the user to access data members directly.

3. Suppose that you didn't know the formula for leap years and didn't have access to the leapYear function above. Write your own function int LeapYear(int y) which returns 1 if the year y is a leap year and 0 if it isn't using only the public functions of the Date class.

4. Implement inline the operator functions += and −= in the class Date. Notice that the −= operator will have two different definitions and that both operators should return an lvalue, that is, their return type should be Date &.

5. The constructor Date(long dS) and the member function setDate(long dS) should probably be made private since they depend on knowing the BASEYEAR, and it would be dangerous to allow the average user to use these functions. Show how to change date.h to accomplish this.

6. Show how to implement operator< and operator<= to compare two Date objects. These should be inline functions in the class returning the integer 1 if the relation is true, 0 if it is false.

7. a) Declare a Person class with two private data members, a name which is a char[20] and a birthday which is a Date. Your class should include a constructor Person(char *, Date) and an accesser, getBirthday().

    b) Show how to declare a Person object HonestAbe whose name is 'Abraham Lincoln' and whose birthday is Feb. 12, 1809.

    c) Write a function int Age(Person) which returns the person's age in number of years. Note that you must distinguish whether the Person's birthday has yet occurred in the current year. You might want to use one of the functions in problem 6.

8. a) The struct tm produced by the standard function localtime also includes the time of day in the fields tm_hour (0 ... 23), tm_min, and tm_sec. Declare a class Time similar to Date which stores the time of day both as hours, minutes, and seconds and as seconds since midnight. There should be two constructors, Time(int hour, int min, int sec) and Time( ), the latter returning the current time. Time should implement the same operators as Date.

b) Declare an enumerated type called AMPM with two values, AM and PM. Add a new constructor to the Time class so that Time(1, 45, 32, PM) would be equivalent to Time(13, 45, 32).

9. (Optional) One of the problems with const declarations mentioned in the footnote on p. 36 is that if you define something like

```
const char *p = "abcdefg";
```

it is hard (for me at least) to remember if it is the pointer or what it points to that is constant. (It is exactly one of the two.) Reason (correctly) which one it should be by remembering that the main purpose of const declarations is to guarantee that const parameters to functions won't be changed by the functions. That is,

```
void bFun( char *p )        // Allows a modification that...

void aFun( const char *p ) // ...doesn't allow
```

6. Introduction to Object-Oriented Programming

At this point we know enough to give a simple example of Object-Oriented Programming using C++. The style of Object-Oriented Programming (OOP) is very different from ordinary programming, and is not appropriate for all types of problems. Typically it is used in a situation in which the program can be seen as several different types of mechanisms (the **objects**) relating to each other. There is generally very little main program, as such: merely enough to initialize the objects and start up the interaction. By the same token, there is considerably less emphasis on top-down programming. The programmer usually starts in a top-down manner, defining each of the object types (in C++, these will be classes) and the actions on these classes (in C++, member functions). Once this is done, the classes and their member functions can be constructed in a bottom-up manner, with little consideration for the implementation of other classes, or even other member functions in the same class. This decomposition of the program into very small, relatively independent pieces makes for greatly simplified programming (if the overall design is done correctly, of course).

We will apply these techniques to the following simple example:

Example 6.1: My mother's TV set and VCR can be controlled with the same remote. Some functions of the remote control apply to both the TV and the VCR, so to determine which, the remote control has a button labeled 'mode' and two lights labeled 'TV' and 'VCR'. Pressing the 'mode' button once causes the light corresponding to the current mode to light briefly. If the 'mode' button is pushed again soon enough, this causes the mode to switch, and *its* corresponding light to light. Our program will simulate this function of the remote by using the 'm' key on the keyboard as the mode switch and displaying our 'lights' on the monitor screen.

The first thing to do in an object-oriented approach is to identify the objects and group similar objects in classes. Then determine the necessary operations on the objects, which will be the member functions in the classes. The traditional method advocated by the literature is to look for nouns in the problem statement, which will correspond to classes, and verbs, which will correspond to operations.

In this case, the nouns are clearly 'light' and 'button'. The 'TV' and 'VCR' light will be class objects of the class 'light' and the mode button will be a class object of the class 'button'. The light class will have one operation, flashing the light, and the button class will have two operations, pushing the button and changing the mode.

The `light` class will have one data member, a character string containing the name of the light, which is what will be displayed when the light is lit. Thus we can declare

```
class light {
  private:
    char name[MAXNAME];
  public:
    light( char *nm ) { strcpy( name, nm ); }
```

```
         //      constructor, with no error checking for name length
       void Flash( void );   // defined in light.cpp
};
```

The general outline of the button class is

```
class button {       // preliminary version
   private:
       data members
   public:
       button( initializing data ) ...
       void Push( void ); // light current light
       void Toggle( void );  // change current light
};
```

The 'mode' button will have two lights associated with it, for 'TV' and 'VCR'. In addition, there must be some indication as to which is the current light. This suggests the following data members:

```
       light choice[2];    // data members for button
       int curChoice;
```

The integer curChoice is a (private) data member since it is important that it always have a legal value (0 or 1) and be changed only by its button. Since the other (unprogrammed) functions of the remote controller will need to know what the choice is, though, we will supply an accesser function for it.

In addition, we need some way of determining whether a sufficiently short time (SHORTTIME) has passed since the last button push, so we need a data member timeOfLastPush. We will assume that a global counter variable Time is maintained elsewhere to compare against. Thus the completed button definition is

```
class button {
   private:
       light choice[2];
       int curChoice;
   public:
       button( char *button0, char *button1 );
       void Push( void );
       void Toggle( void );
       int current( void ) { return curChoice; }
};
```

Now we are ready to complete the class definitions. Let us assume that we have a function Delay() which will be used to delay some short length of time, the amount of time that a light will flash on. We will put the prototype for Delay() into light.h and its definition in light.cpp. This is not because it is part of the light class but because it is *necessary* to the light class and we want to make the light class easy to reuse in other applications. Also by using #ifndef, we can allow the user to define a maximum length for light names and the length of the delay or use our default definitions. The complete files for `light` are

```cpp
// light.h -- declaration of the light class

#include <string.h>

#ifndef MAXNAME
#define MAXNAME 10
#endif

#ifndef DELAYCOUNT
#define DELAYCOUNT 200000L // determine experimentally
      // this is about right for a 33Mhz 486
#endif

void Delay( void );

class light {
   private:
      char name[MAXNAME];
   public:
      light( char *nm ) { strcpy( name, nm ); }
         //    constructor, with no error checking for name length
      void Flash( void );
};

// light.cpp -- implementation of the light class

#include "light.h"
#include <iostream.h>

void light::Flash( void )
{
   cout << name << flush;
   Delay( );
   for ( int i = strlen( name ); i > 0; --i)
      cout << "\b \b" << flush; // erase each character of name
            // in turn with backspace, blank, backspace
}

void Delay( void )
{
   long i = DELAYCOUNT;

   while( i-- > 0 ) ; // do nothing!
}
```

Note that the `flush` stream manipulator must be used here on C++'s that buffer input since there will be no `cins` or `endls` in the program, as otherwise nothing would appear. (See p. 8 for an explanation.)

The code for the `button` class is

```cpp
// button.h -- declaration of the button class
```

```
#include "light.h"

class button {
   private:
      light *choice[2];
      int curChoice;
   public:
      button( char * button0, char * button1 );
      void Push( void );
      void Toggle( void ) { curChoice = 1 - curChoice; }
      int current( void ) { return curChoice; }
};

// button.cpp -- implementation of the button class

#include "button.h"

button::button( char *button0, char *button1 )
{
   choice[0] = light(button0);
   choice[1] = light(button1);
   curChoice = 0;
}

void button::Push( void )
{
   choice[curChoice] -> Flash( );
}
```

The definitions of remote.h and the main program, remote.cpp, are now quite simple:

```
// remote.h -- global declarations for the remote control

#define MAXNAME ...      // if you wish to redefine it
#define DELAYCOUNT ...   // can redefine here too
#define SHORTTIME 5

// remote.cpp -- implementation of remote control

#include <conio.h> // for keyboard function prototypes
#include "remote.h"
#include "button.h"

long Time = 0;
long timeOfLastPush = Time - (SHORTTIME + 1);
   // so that the first push will
   //  of necessity be after a long time!

button mode( "TV", "VCR" );

void main( void )
{
   for (;;) { // a 'standard' infinite loop
```

```
        if ( kbhit( ) )
          switch ( getch( ) ) { // get keystroke with no echo
    case 'm': if ( timeOfLastPush + SHORTTIME >= Time )
                 mode.Toggle();
              timeOfLastPush = Time;
              mode.Push( );
              break;
    case 'q': return;
           // other remote functions could be inserted here
           }
        else Delay( );      // so each iteration of the loop takes
                       // approximately the same time
        ++ Time;
    }
}
```

Here we have made use of functions available in both Borland and Microsoft Visual C++ for determining if a key has been hit without reading it (kbhit ()) and reading and returning an input character without echoing it (getch ()). Timing is accomplished by having each pass through the main for loop take approximately the time of the Delay () call. That's the reason we don't simply use getch() to wait for a keystroke — if we did we wouldn't know how long we had waited without getting into further complications of looking at the time clock.

Exercises 6

1.   Generalize the button class so that it can cycle through n lights. The constructor function could be declared as button(int n, char * nm[]), where nm is now an array of n character strings, the names of the successive lights controlled by the button. Whenever a button push causes curChoice to change, it changes to (curChoice + 1) % n; i.e., curChoice cycles through 0, 1, 2, ..., n–1, 0, 1, ...

2.   Make the light class more generally useful by adding the public member functions On and Off, which will be used by Flash.

3.   Write an object oriented version of the coin and change part of a vending machine. The machine will have three objects: (1) a slot, which accepts coins in the form of keystrokes from the keyboard: 'n' for nickel, 'd' for dime, and 'q' for quarter; (2) a change dispenser, which collects the nickels inserted and dispenses change of up to four nickels when sufficient coins have been inserted to cover the PRICE of the item dispensed; and (3) a light which shows 'Exact Change Only' when the change maker is unable to make change, i.e., when the change maker contains fewer than four nickels. For the last, use the light class as modified in Exercise 2 above. As a refinement, your slot could also accept the character 'r' for the coin return, and nickels inserted wouldn't be transferred to the change maker until an item had been dispensed. This Exercise has purposely been left a little vague, to give you several things to consider in the design of the classes.

7. More on Operator Overloading

7.1 Overloading the << and >> Operators

The operators >> and << are used in C as the right and left shift operators. As you may have guessed by now, the use of these operators with `cout` and `cin` constitutes an overloading of them. In fact, `iostream.h` declares two classes, `istream` (input stream) and `ostream` (output stream), of which `cin` and `cout` are class objects, respectively. In `ostream` for instance, there are several declarations to overload the operator <<:

```
someType operator << ( int x );    // overloading << in ostream
someType operator << ( real x );
someType operator << ( char c );
someType operator << ( char * s );
    etc.
```

The next question is what should the type *someType* be? It would seem that the << operation doesn't produce a useful value, so perhaps `void` is the right choice. However, let us examine a statement like

```
cout << a << b << c << d << ...
```

Just as C would parenthesize an expression like u + v + w + x + y as (((u + v) + w) + x) + y, C++ parenthesizes `cout << a << b << c << d << ...` as

```
...(((cout << a) << b) << c) << d ...
```

Therefore the *result* of applying the function `cout << a` must be something we want to put on the left side of << b to get the output to continue. Clearly we want to send b to `cout` too, so the value of `cout << a` must be `cout` — the actual `cout`, not a copy. The *someType* is `ostream` & The typical `operator <<` declaration should be

```
ostream & operator << ( anyType x );
       // overloading << in ostream
```

and the definition would be

```
ostream & ostream::operator << ( anyType x )
{     // overloading << from within ostream
      ...
   return *this ;
}
```

With any class designed for general use, one should declare an overloading of the << and >> operators so that class objects can be input and output via streams. The principles of information hiding say we shouldn't go back and modify an already-existing, working, standard system piece such as `iostream`. Luckily we don't have to, as operator overloadings don't have to be class member functions. (That is what allows us to overload an operator when the first operand isn't a class object but the second is.) In this case we write a regular function declaration in which *both* operands are listed explicitly:

```
ostream & operator << ( ostream & os , anyType x );
        // overloading << OUTSIDE ostream
```

and the actual function definition becomes

standard form of
stream <<
overload

```
ostream & operator << ( ostream & os, anyType x )
{      // overloading << from OUTSIDE ostream
    ...
    return os ;
}
```

The `operator <<` function for `Date` should have its declaration included in `date.h` as it is logically associated with `Date`s, and its definition in `date.cpp` for the same reason. The code is

```
// date.h -- ...

class Date {
    ...
};    // end of declaration of class Date

ostream & operator << ( ostream & os, Date & d );

// date.cpp
    ...
ostream & operator << ( ostream & os, Date & d )
{
    os << d.getMonth() << "/" << d.getDay() << "/" << d.getYear();
    return os;
}
```

Then the code

```
Date Happy(6, 11, 83);
    ...
cout << Happy << endl;
```

produces the output

```
6/11/1983
```

Exercises 7.1

1. Write the code to overload the operator >> so that it can be used to input a Date. On input, a Date is assumed to be an integer (the month) followed by exactly one non-blank character followed by another integer (the day) followed by exactly one non-blank character, followed by the year.

2. Write a '<<' operator for the Time class introduced in Exercise 5.2–85. Declare a variable TimeStyle outside the class. The Time is to be displayed in the style 13:42:27 if TimeStyle is 24, and otherwise in the form 1:42:27 PM.

7.2 Complex Numbers

This section will be used to refine our ideas about operator functions. We will develop a class to represent the complex numbers, which we will use in the next section to write a program to draw the Mandelbrot set. (Many implementations of C++ include an implementation of complex numbers. We will develop our own, however.)

The square root of –1, denoted i, is introduced in order to be able to solve the equation $x^2 + 1 = 0$. In order to be able to do algebra with i, we consider the set of **complex numbers**, the formal objects $x + yi$ where x and y are any real numbers.[6] With the obvious definitions, we can add, subtract, and multiply complex numbers and get other complex numbers:[7]

adding, subtracting, and multiplying complex numbers

$$(x + iy) \pm (u + vi) = (x \pm u) + (y \pm v)i$$

$$(x + yi) \cdot (u + vi) = xu + (xv + yu)i + yvi^2$$

$$= (xu - yv) + (xv + yu)i$$

Less obviously, we can divide one complex number by another and obtain a complex number. If $z = x + yi$ is a complex number, the **real part** of z is $Re(z) = x$, the **imaginary part** of z is $Im(z) = y$, and the **complex conjugate** $\bar{z}$ of z is defined as $x - yi$. Then the **absolute value** of z is $|z| = \sqrt{z\bar{z}} = \sqrt{x^2 + y^2}$. Formally, we can divide z by $w = u + vi$ as follows:

dividing complex numbers

$$\frac{z}{w} = \frac{z}{w} \cdot \frac{\bar{w}}{\bar{w}} = \frac{z \cdot \bar{w}}{|w|^2} = (xu + yv)|w|^{-2} + (xv - yu)|w|^{-2}i$$

assuming that $w \neq 0 = 0 + 0i$.

---

[6]It is truly amazing that when we add this one root of one equation to the reals to get the complex numbers, not only do we get roots of all polynomials with *real* coefficients, we get roots of all polynomials with *complex* coefficients!

[7]If you are allergic to algebra, you can simply accept the formulas we develop here and skip down to the definition of the complex class.

Thus we can define the header file for the `complex` class with the data members being the real and imaginary parts of the complex number:

```
// complex.h -- defines complex class

#include <iostream.h>

class complex {
  private:
    double real_part, imag_part;
  public:
    // constructor
    complex( double re = 0, double im = 0 )
          { real_part = re; imag_part = im; }

    // accessers
    double getReal( void ) { return real_part; }
    double getImag( void ) { return imag_part; }

    complex operator + ( complex z );
    complex operator - ( complex z );
    complex operator * ( complex z );
    complex operator / ( complex z );
};

ostream & operator << ( ostream & os, complex z );

extern complex I;  // defined in complex.cpp as complex(0, 1)
// capital I is used instead of lower case i as the latter is
// often used for a loop index, and I is more visible
```

Addition can easily be defined as an inline function:

```
complex operator + ( complex z )
       { return complex( real_part + z.real_part,
                   imag_part + z.imag_part ); }
```

With ordinary numbers, there are two '−' operations, *binary* minus, such as x − y, which we declared above, and *unary* minus, such as −x. C++ will distinguish between these two operations and allow us to overload both:

```
complex operator - ( complex z )        // binary -
       { return *this + ( -z ); }        // uses unary -
complex operator - ( void )      // unary -
       { return complex( -real_part, -imag_part ); }
```

We can get the operation of complex conjugation by overloading the (unary) complement operator '~' as follows:

```
complex operator ~ ( void )
          { return complex( real_part, -imag_part ); }
```

and in order to make it easier to compute the quotient of two complex numbers, we add the non-member function

```
double abssq( complex z ); // square of absolute value
```

To allow us to use Re(z) and Im(z) for the real and imaginary parts of z like the mathematicians do, we will also define the non-member functions

```
inline double Re( complex z ) { return z.getReal(); }
inline double Im( complex z ) { return z.getImag(); }
```

This may seem like a lot of overhead, calling Re which calls getReal just to get the value of a variable. Remember however that both Re and getReal are inline functions, so the code generated should be the same as if we could access real_part directly.

Multiplication and division can be done in complex.cpp, which starts off as follows:

```
// complex.cpp -- definitions for the complex class

#include "complex.h"

complex I(0, 1);

ostream & operator << ( ostream & os, complex & z )
{
   if ( Re(z) != 0 || Im(z) == 0 ) {
      os << Re(z);
      if ( Im(z) > 0 )
         os << '+';
   }
   if ( Im(z) != 0 ) {
      if (z.Im() == -1)
         os << '-';
      else
         if (Im(z) != 1)
            os << Im(z);
      os << 'i';
   }
   return os;
}

complex complex::operator * ( complex z )
{
   return complex(
            real_part * z.real_part - imag_part * z.imag_part,
            real_part * z.imag_part + imag_part * z.real_part
   );
}

double abssq( complex z )
{
   return Re(z) * Re(z) + Im(z) * Im(z);
```

```
        }

        complex complex::operator / ( complex z )
        {
            complex w = (*this) * (~ z);
            double modsq = abssq( z );

            return complex( w.x / modsq, w.y / modsq );
        }
```

The '<<' operator is a little tricky so that we can get the usual simplifications:

```
        cout << complex( 0, 0 );    // displays '0'
        cout << complex( 5, 0 );    // displays '5'
        cout << complex( 0, 5 );    // displays '5i'
        cout << complex( 3, 5 );    // displays '3+5i'
        cout << complex( 3, -5 );     // displays '3-5i'
        cout << complex( 3, 1 );    // displays '3+i'
        cout << complex( 3, -1 );     // displays '3-i'
            etc.
```

You may wonder why the arithmetic operator functions aren't declared with reference parameters, given the Rule of Thumb on p. 39. The explanation is a bit devious:

mechanism for casting ints and floats to complex

In numeric expressions in C, data types can be mixed, with C choosing the 'most comprehensive' data type and converting everything to that type. Thus if we write '1.2 + 3', C will convert everything to `double` (since C does all real arithmetic in double precision). Clearly it would be useful if the same thing would happen with `complex` objects in C++. We would like to be able to write 'z + 1' for z complex and have automatic conversion of '1' to complex. In fact this happens!

When C++ attempts to evaluate z + 1 = z.operator+(1) for complex z, it looks over its possibilities for an `operator+` with first operand complex. The only possibility also has second operand complex, so it looks to see if it can make a `complex` object out of '1'; that is, it looks at the constructors for `complex`. The only one it has with a single argument is `complex( double )` (the second parameter defaults to 0), and even C can cast an `int` to a `double`. Therefore '1' becomes `complex( 1, 0 )` and the addition takes place as we would hope.

If we declare `complex operator +( complex &z )`, some C++'s will go ahead and cast the resulting `complex(1)` to type `complex &` (!) by constructing a temporary containing `complex(1)` and passing a reference to it. However, some won't. For a discussion of this phenomenon, see 'A Cautionary Tale' in the Preface.

The same automatic cast also works for the other operators, *as long as the non-complex value comes second!*

casting the left operand to complex requires another function

So what happens with '1 + z'? Since '1' isn't a class object, we would have to fall back on C evaluation of expressions to force a type-change of '1', and C knows nothing about `complex` objects. The solution is simple, if a bit tedious. We must overload the standard operators yet again by defining `complex operator θ (` `double, complex )` functions for θ equal to each of the four operators +, −, *, and /. This is done in `complex.h`, so that they will be available to any program using complex numbers, but outside the class since the first argument of the function isn't a complex object. The final form of `complex.h` is

```
// complex.h -- defines complex class

#include <iostream.h>

class complex {
   private:
      double real_part, imag_part;
   public:
      // constructor
      complex( double re = 0, double im = 0 )
         { real_part = re; imag_part = im; }

      // accessers
      double getReal( void ) { return real_part; }
      double getImag( void ) { return imag_part; }

      complex operator + ( complex z )
         { return complex( real_part + z.real_part,
                           imag_part + z.imag_part ); }
      complex operator - () // unary minus
         { return complex( -real_part, -imag_part ); }
      complex operator - ( complex z )        // binary minus
         { return *this + (- z); }
      complex operator * ( complex z );
      complex operator / ( complex z );
      complex operator ~ ( void ) // complex conjugate
         { return complex( real_part, - imag_part ); }
};

extern complex I;

inline double Re( complex z ) { return z.getReal(); }
inline double Im( complex z ) { return z.getImag(); }

   // The following operators are necessary because C++ can coerce
   // complex + double properly, but not double + complex, etc.

inline complex operator + ( double x, complex z )
        { return z + x; }
inline complex operator - ( double x, complex z )
        { return - z + x; }
inline complex operator * ( double x, complex z )
        { return z * x; }
inline complex operator / ( double x, complex z )
        { return complex( x ) / z; }

ostream & operator << ( ostream & os, complex z );
double abssq( complex & z );
```

Exercises 7.2

1.   Review Question: Why can we use `z.real_part` in the coding for `operator * ` and `/` but must use `Re(z)` in `abssq` and `operator <<`?

2.   a)   My original version of `operator / ( complex )` was as follows:

```
complex complex::operator / ( complex z )
{
    return *this * ~z / abssq( z );
}
```

which caused an infinite loop. Why?

   b)   Even though the class member functions for `operator*` and `operator/` work if the second argument is a `double`, they aren't as efficient as if special purpose functions had been written for this purpose. (The `complex` version converts the second argument to `complex` and then does a more complicated `complex` multiplication or division than is necessary.) Write inline member functions for the operators as follows:

```
operator * ( double d ) { ... }
operator / ( double d ) { ... }
```

Notice that if we have made these definitions, the function in part a) will work properly.

3.   For some applications, it is more convenient to represent complex numbers in *polar coordinates*. The complex number $z = x + yi$ can be represented in polar coordinates as (r, θ) where $z = r\cos\theta + ir\sin\theta$ and $r = |z|$, $\theta = \arctan\frac{y}{x}$, which can be computed in C with the function `atan2(y, x)` from the include file `math.h`. r is called the *modulus* and θ the *argument* of the complex number i.

   a)   Write member functions `mod()` and `arg()` which return the modulus and argument, respectively, of a complex number.

   b)   Polar coordinate representations of complex numbers are particularly useful when looking at multiplication because `(z1*z2).mod() = (z1.mod()) * (z2.mod())` and `(z1*z2).arg() = z1.arg() + z2.arg()`. Use these facts to write an overloaded version of the square root function `sqrt` that finds one of the square roots of a complex number.

4.   Write an overloading of the stream operator '`>>`' for complex numbers. Assume that on input, the number is in one of four forms: `x?`, `yi`, `x+yi`, or `x-yi`. `x` and `y` are assumed to be `int`, `float`, or `double` numbers and `?` represents an indifferent character, which can be discarded.

5.   a)   Design and implement a class `Rational` to represent rational numbers. A rational number is the quotient of two (long) integers, p/q, $q \neq 0$. Arrange it so that

the data members p and q (or num and denom?) are always in lowest terms and q > 0. That is, divide out by their greatest common divisor. (See almost any programming book for a method.) The constructor could have q default to 1, and p to 0. It should be possible to add, subtract, multiply, and divide Rational objects with each other, as well as with integers on either side.

b)   Develop a version of << for the Rational class. If the denominator is 1, don't print out the '/1' part.

c)   Develop a version of >> for the Rational class. A Rational number is assumed to be an integer followed by the character '/' followed by another integer, with no intervening blanks.

d)   Write routines to overload the operators '<' and '<=' so that they apply to Rational objects. a/b < c/d precisely when ad < bc. (Remember that we are assuming that b and d are greater than 0.)

e)   As we have seen, type conversions *to* a class type are normally taken care of by the class constructor functions. (int + Date would be taken care of by overloading '+'.) It is also possible to **overload a type cast function** in order to convert *from* a class type to another type. For instance, overload the double type cast by defining a member function operator double() in the Rational class. Then if r is of type Rational, we can write expressions like 1.0 + r and (double)r or double(r).

this technique doesn't work for 1 + z, z complex. Why?

f)   It can be shown that any positive rational number can be written in the following form:

$$\frac{1}{n_1}+\frac{1}{n_2}+\cdots+\frac{1}{n_k}$$

where $n_1 < n_2 < \ldots < n_k$ are positive integers and equality is *exact*. Thus for example,

$$2\frac{1}{2}=\frac{5}{2}=\frac{1}{1}+\frac{1}{2}+\frac{1}{3}+\frac{1}{4}+\frac{1}{5}+\frac{1}{6}+\frac{1}{20}$$

(The ancient Egyptians represented non-whole numbers this way, because they believed that there was only *one* 1/4, for instance, so 1/4 + 1/4 = 1/4 as far as they were concerned. Note that the representation is far from unique: 1/2 = 1/3 + 1/6 = 1/4 + 1/5 + 1/20 = ...) Using the Rational class, write a program that takes as input a rational number m/n and produces as output such a representation. (Use cout for output.) Method: Start with d = 1 and increment d until 1/d <= m/n. Replace m/n by m/n - 1/d, output 1/d, increment d, and continue until m/n = 0. Note that it is necessary to have exact arithmetic for this method to work — it wouldn't work with doubles instead of Rationals as a double can't represent most fractions exactly.

7.3 A Fun Break: Mandelbrot Sets

This section will use the `complex` class developed in section 7.2 for drawing all or part of the **Mandelbrot set**. This example isn't at all central to our discussion of C++ and can easily be skipped, though you might want to take a look at the paragraphs on string streams.

The Mandelbrot set is one of the most common examples of **fractal geometry**, which has become quite popular in recent years both in recreational computer science and in serious, realistic computer graphics. To do the program, we will need some simple concepts of computer graphics.

a quick intro to computer graphics

The graphics monitor screen is divided up into individual dots, called **pixels**, which is short for picture elements. Typical VGA monitors have a grid of 640 (horizontal) by 480 (vertical) pixels. A pixel is located by its integer **screen coordinates** (p, q) which are numbered from 0 in the upper left-hand corner (or sometimes, as in analytic geometry, from the lower left-hand corner). Colors for pixels are numbered from 0, which is normally black, up to some constant MAXCOLOR that is usually $2^n - 1$ for some n. (For a monochrome screen, MAXCOLOR is 1.) We will assume we are given a function `putpixel(p, q, c)` which colors pixel (p, q) with color c. `putpixel` and a few other functions are special to Borland C++. Similar functions are available with Microsoft Visual C++. The version of the program on the disk that comes with this book will compile properly with either compiler.

Sample VGA Screen Coordinates

Returning to the problem at hand, we note that a complex number $z = x + yi$ can be associated with a point (x, y) in the plane. We also use complex numbers denoted by λ (the Greek letter *lambda*) instead of z, and if $\lambda = \mu + vi$ we can just as easily associate λ with the point (μ, v). (μ and v are the Greek letters *mu* and *nu*.) The point $\lambda = (\mu, v)$ is related to the real-world situation we are graphing, and is said to be in **world coordinates**, which can be positive or negative numbers with fractional parts. One of our problems will be to convert between world coordinates and screen coordinates.

To determine whether or not any 'point' λ is in the Mandelbrot set, we look at the behavior of the following process: z is initially set to λ, and then we repeatedly replace z by $z^2 + \lambda$. One of two things will happen. Either eventually $|z|$ will get larger and larger, or it will stay below some constant (dependent on λ). If it stays bounded, we say that λ is in the Mandelbrot set. The following is pseudocode for determining if λ is in the Mandelbrot set:

```
z = lambda;
for ( int ct = 1; ct < REPLIM &&
                        abssq( z ) < SIZELIM; ++ct )
    z = z * z + lambda;
if ( ct < REPLIM ) // lambda isn't in set
    color screen pixel corresponding to lambda white;
```

```
else              // lambda is in set
    color screen pixel corresponding to lambda black;
```

A little experimentation shows that taking REPLIM = 20 and SIZELIM = 4 produces reasonable results. We can make the picture much more interesting if we color the outside pixels according to the number of iterations necessary to make abssq(z) >= SIZELIM. Also, we will start with *all* pixels colored black. The coloring part then becomes

```
if ( ct < REPLIM ) // lambda isn't in set
    putpixel( p, q, ct % (MAXCOLOR + 1) );
```

To draw the entire Mandelbrot set, we will embed the statements above in nested for loops. One will go through the p screen coordinate and one will go through the q screen coordinate.

```
for ( int p = 0; p <= MAX; ++i )
    for ( int q = 0; q <= MAX; ++j ) {
        z = lambda = toWC( p, q );
        ...
    }
```

The function toWC turns screen coordinates into complex number world coordinates. We are making our picture square, and smaller than full-screen to speed up the program. Once a couple of constants are computed, toWC is quite simple:

```
double factor;       // screen-to-world multiplier
complex addend;      // screen-to-world shifter

complex toWC( int p, int q )
{
    return (complex( p, -q ) + addend) * factor;
}
```

The minus sign on q is because our vertical screen coordinates grow from the top down while world coordinates (analytic geometry) grow from the bottom up.

Since we are usually most interested in the center of a picture of (part of) the Mandelbrot set, we will let the user specify the center *(x0, y0)*, and side *s* in world coordinates. Clearly factor = *s*/MAX and the upper left-hand corner (0, 0) goes to world coordinates $(x0 - s/2, y0 + s/2)$, so (0 + addend) * factor = addend * s / MAX = complex($x0, y0$) + s * complex(-.5, .5), hence addend = MAX * (complex($x0, y0$)/s + complex(-.5, .5)).

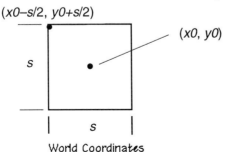

$(x0-s/2, y0+s/2)$

$(x0, y0)$

s

s

World Coordinates

'I/O' to and from character strings

X0, *y0*, and *s* will come from the command line arguments `argc` and `argv[]`. We will convert from character strings to `doubles` using **string streams**, which are the stream I/O equivalent of `sscanf`. String streams take their input from or write their output to character strings rather than the user's terminal. The `istrstream( char * s, int len )` constructor creates an input string stream which 'reads' and translates characters from the characters string `s` and `ostrstream( char *s, int len )` creates an output string stream which 'writes' formatted data into the character string `s`. `len` is the length of `s`, not including the terminating null character '\0'. To use string streams, we must include the file `strstream.h` as well as `iostream.h`. Thus we could code

```
#include <iostream.h>
#include <strstream.h>
    ...
char sout[101], *sin = "2.2";
double d;
istrstream strin( sin, sizeof( sin ) );
        // input string stream strin
ostrstream strout( sout, 100 );
        // output string stream strout

strin >> d;                 // sets d = 2.2
strout << d + 1;    // sets sout = "3.2"
```

In the program below, we need input string streams only briefly, one for each `argv`, so we create them as 'constant' string streams that are destroyed as soon as their usage is ended.

The program uses Borland C++ graphics procedures, assumes 16 color VGA, and does no error checking. The program is rather slow, so the inner loop includes a call to the `kbhit()`, introduced in Chapter 6, which allows you to hit a key and stop execution of the program. To get all of the interesting part of the Mandelbrot set, execute

```
mandel -0.75 0 2.5
```

($x0 = -0.75$, $y0 = 0$, and the square side = 2.5.) Interesting details can be viewed by moving the center and taking a much smaller side. The program follows, with the parts actually making use of complex numbers and string streams in **bold face**.

```
// mandel.cpp -- draw the mandelbrot set or parts thereof

#include <graphics.h> // special to Borland C++
#include <conio.h>
#include <stdio.h>
#include "complex.h"
#include <strstream.h>
        // iostream.h already included through complex.h

#define REPLIM 20
#define SIZELIM 4
```

```
#define MAXCOLOR 15

#define MAX 400     // number of pixels per side

double x0, y0, side;  // center x and y coordinates and side size
                      // in world coordinates
double factor;        // screen-to-world multiplier
complex addend;       // screen-to-world shifter

complex toWC( int i, int j )
{
   return (complex( i, -j ) + addend) * factor;
}

double getdouble( char * s )
{
   double d;

   istrstream( s, sizeof( s ) ) >> d;
   return d;
}

int main( int argc, char * argv[] )
{
   complex lambda, z;
   int gD = DETECT, gM;     // special to Borland C++

   if ( argc != 4 ) {
      cerr << "usage: mandel x-center y-center side" << endl;
      return 1;
      }
   x0 = getdouble( argv[1] );
   y0 = getdouble( argv[2] );
   side = getdouble( argv[3] );

   factor = side / MAX;
   addend = MAX * (complex( x0, y0 ) / side +
            complex( -0.5, 0.5 ));

   initgraph ( &gD, &gM, "c:\\bc4\\bgi" );
           // special to Borland C++

   for ( int p = 0;  p <= MAX; ++p )
      for ( int q = 0;  q <= MAX; ++q ) {
         z = lambda = toWc( p, q );
         for ( int ct = 1; ct < REPLIM &&
                             abssq( z ) < SIZELIM; ++ct )
             z = z * z + lambda;
         if ( ct < REPLIM )
            putpixel( p, q, ct % (MAXCOLOR + 1) );
         if ( kbhit() ) return 0;
         }
   getch();
   return 0;
}
```

The figure shows the output of the execution mandel -0.75 0 2.5 when only black and white are used, by replacing the putpixel call above with

```
putpixel( p, q, (ct & 1) ? MAXCOLOR : 1 );
   // monochrome Mandelbrot set
   // ct & 1 is 'true' if ct is odd. MAXCOLOR is white
```

The large blob in the center with the lobes and hairy fringes is the Mandelbrot set and the wavy black and white bands around it represent the various iterations at which $z^2 + \lambda$ "escapes".

Exercise 7.3

1.   To form the Mandelbrot set, we varied λ and plotted whether or not $z^2 + \lambda$ "escapes". We can on the other hand hold λ fixed and vary the initial z and get a **Julia Set**. An interesting example is obtained if we hold $\lambda = -0.544 - 0.54*I$ fixed and plot initial z values over the square centered at (0, 0) and 3 on a side. I got the most interesting results by taking REPLIM = 60, SIZELIM = 6, and making all of the points outside the set (i.e. the points for which $z^2 + \lambda$ escapes) the same color.

8. Classes that Allocate Memory

Many important classes contain data members that are pointers to memory allocated by the class objects. We will show an example of such a class in section 8.1. In C and similar languages, many problems can be caused when pointers aren't properly initialized or the memory they point to is improperly disposed of. We will discuss two ways in which C++ copes with these problems, *destructors* and *copy constructors*, in sections 8.2 and 8.3. The copy constructor is a fairly advanced technique and section 8.3 can be omitted on first reading.

8.1 An Example Class that Allocates Memory

We're going to create a simple singly-linked list implementation of a stack. Each node on the stack/list will be a class object of the form

'info' is the data contained in the node and `link` points to the next node in the list. (We call the list 'singly-linked' because there is only one link field. We will discuss doubly linked lists in Chapter 10.) The beginnings of the declaration will be as follows:

```
// link1.h -- list nodes with one link

class link1 {
   private:
      double info;  // example info
      link1 *link;
   public:
      // constructors
      link1( double newitem = 0 )
         { info = newitem; link = NULL; }
         ...
      // accessers
      double getInfo( void ) { return info; }
      link1 *getLink( void ) { return link; }
   ...
};
```

The stack will consist of one `link1` object, the **stack head**, which will always be there, and various stack items that can be added (*push*ed). The stack head is declared by

```
link1 stack( -1.0 );  // info in stack head doesn't matter
// -1.0 used to indicate stack head in figures
```

which appears in memory as follows:

The gray 'X' indicates the that link = NULL, i.e., that this is the end of the list. The situation pictured above is an *empty* stack. If we then 'push' the numbers 1.1 and 2.2 onto the stack, it will appear as follows:

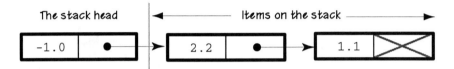

To 'push' a new item onto the stack, such as the float number 3.3 means to insert a list class object with info 3.3 between the list head and the items on the stack:

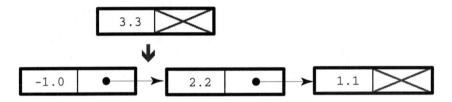

This involves resetting pointers as follows:

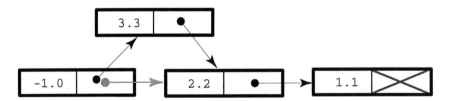

To do this, we create a new member function in link1.h:

```
void push( double item ); // '*this' is the stack head.
```

with implementation in link1.cpp:

```
void link1::push( double item )
{
    link1 *l = new link1( item );

    l -> link = link;
    link = l;
}
```

We can produce the stack in the last diagram above with the following main program:

```
#include "link1.h"

void main( void )
{
   list stack( -1.0 );        // list head

   stack.push( 1.1 );
   stack.push( 2.2 );
   stack.push( 3.3 ); // Now -1.0 ==> 3.3 ==> 2.2 ==> 1.1
}
```

Exercises 8.1

1.   A **binary tree** is a finite set of objects, called **nodes**, which is either empty or which can be partitioned into three subsets: one consisting of a single node — the **root** of the tree — and two binary trees called the **left and right subtrees**. For example the figure below is a binary tree. We partition it into three subsets, A, the root, {B, D, E} the left subtree, and {C, F, G} the right subtree. We then have to apply the definition recursively. The left subtree is a binary tree because it can be partitioned into a root, B, a left subtree {D}, and a right subtree {E}. {D} and {E} are binary trees consisting of a root and empty left and right subtrees.

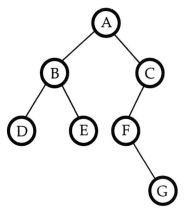

Similarly one can show that {C, F, B} is a binary tree. The roots of the left and right subtrees are called the **left and right child**, respectively, of the root of the tree. Thus in the diagram above, B and C are the left and right children of A.

You are to construct an implementation of the ADT 'binary tree' (operations to be defined below) using a class btree. Each node will be a btree object. The information in each node will be Name, a char* pointer to a string allocated with new and each object will contain pointers lchild and rchild to the left and right children. Thus we could picture a btree object as follows:

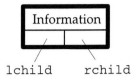

lchild   rchild

Your class should have the following member functions:

a) A constructor that takes as its parameter a string of characters, allocates storage for the characters in the class object and copies the parameter string into this storage. The parameter should default to the empty string, giving a default constructor.

b) An overload of the << operator. When root is a btree object, cout << root causes the tree to be printed in **inorder**, that is, first the lchild is printed, then root information, then the rchild. Printing the information in root consists of printing the character string followed by a blank. Printing the children involves applying the << operation recursively. If proot points to the btree in the figure in part d) of this exercise, cout << *proot displays the names in alphabetical order.

c) An overload of the operator== function that returns 1 (true) if two btrees have the same structure and information but don't necessarily occupy the same memory. This function is also recursive.

d) A **binary search tree** is a binary tree with the additional property that for each object in the tree, all the information strings in the lchild subtree are less than the information in the root, which in turn is less than all the information strings in the rchild subtree. Create a member function Insert such that if proot points to the root of a binary search tree, proot -> Insert(character string) inserts a node containing *character string* in its proper place in the binary search tree. Thus if we inserted the signs of the Zodiac in their usual order Aries, Taurus, Gemini, Cancer, Leo, Virgo, Libra, Scorpio, Sagittarius, Capricorn, Aquarius, and Pisces, using code such as the following:

```
btree *proot = NULL;     // Note: no constructor called

    proot -> Insert( "Aries" );
    proot -> Insert( "Taurus" );
        . . .
    proot -> Insert( "Pisces" );
```

we would get the binary search tree

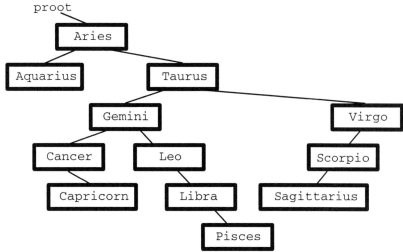

If we then executed

```
cout << *proot << endl;
```

we would display the signs of the Zodiac in alphabetical order.

8.2 Destructors

Every class object has memory allocated for it when the object is created and deallocated when the object is destroyed. If the object is a local variable, this memory is automatically allocated (usually on a runtime stack) on entry to the variable's scope and automatically deallocated on exit. For class objects allocated by new, the memory is explicitly allocated by new and explicitly deallocated by delete. But what happens to memory *pointed to* by data members when the object ceases to exist? The allocated memory may no longer be accessible, but still takes up space. This is a frequent source of errors in C programs.

To see to it that memory *pointed to* by data members is deallocated reliably, a new type of member function called the **destructor** is used. Whenever a class object is destroyed its destructor function is called just before the memory for its data members is deleted. The destructor can then perform whatever cleanup it likes, most importantly, deleting any allocated memory its data members point to.

The declaration for the (unique) class destructor is in the form ~*classname* (void) — no parameters or returned value must be given. In link1.h we can declare the destructor

```
~link1( void );
```

with implementation in link1.cpp

```
link1::~link1( void )
{
```

```
            cout << "destroying " << info << endl;
                // for demonstration purposes
            delete link;
    }
```

Consider the `main()` program on p. 67 that pushes 1.1, 2.2, and 3.3 onto a stack. When `main()` is exited, we leave the scope of the variable `stack` and it is destroyed. C++ generates a call to `stack.~link1()`. Three actions are then performed: (1) the line "`destroying  -1.0`" is displayed, (2) `delete` is performed on the `link1` object containing 3.3, and (3) the memory containing the `info` and `link` fields of `stack` is deleted (implicitly). The `delete` operation in (2) causes `~link1()` to be called again (recursively) with `this` pointing to the object containing 3.3. That call results in the three actions (2.1) the line "`destroying 3.3`" is displayed, (2.2) `delete` is performed on the `link1` object containing 2.2, and (3) the memory containing the `info` and `link` fields of the node containing 2.2 is deleted. Continuing this way, we will add steps (2.2.1–3) to delete the node containing 1.1, and ultimately, the following is displayed:

```
destroying -1.0
destroying 3.3
destroying 2.2
destroying 1.1
```

When we get to the point of deleting NULL, (2.2.2), the chain of `~link1()` calls is terminated and we exit back up the chain, deleting in turn the memory for the objects containing 1.1, 2.2, then 3.3, then –1.0. The built-in `delete` operation is used on the nodes containing 1.1, 2.2, and 3.3, and the implicit delete of a local variable is used on `stack`, the node containing –1.0.

For the `link1` destructor to work properly, all items on a list other than the first must have been created with new. Suppose we could write

```
    link1 a, b;
        ...
    a.link = &b;  // ILLEGAL; link is a private data member
        ...
```

Then when the destructor for a was called, it would attempt to `delete  &b`, an error. Luckily the class protection mechanism rules out this problem.

Exercises 8.2

1. Write code for a `link1` member function

```
    void init_stack( void )
```

which deletes all nodes *following* the node it is applied to, and sets the `link1` field of its own object to NULL. Note that this may result in the destructor function being called.

2. a) Write a destructor function for the `btree` class as described in Exercise 8.1–1.

b) Suppose we add to the destructor the following first line:

```
cout << "Destroying " << Name << endl;
```

If we destroyed `*proot` in the tree pictured in Exercise 8.1–1(d), what sequence of messages would be displayed?

3. Write a `link1` member function `float pop()` such that `stack.pop()` returns the info of the first item on `stack` other than the stack head and removes and deletes the node containing it. (Carefully! Assume that the destructor exists.) Thus if the list contained `-1.0  3.3  2.2  1.1` before `pop`, `pop` would return `3.3` and the list would then contain `-1.0  2.2  1.1`.

8.3 Copy Constructors

Another problem that arises with classes that allocate memory is what to do when copying an object of such a class. Copying happens when a class object is passed as a value parameter or is declared as equal to another class object.

```
void aFun( classtype A )    // Note: value parameter
{
    ...
}

classtype B, C = B;   // C is a copy of B
    ...
    aFun( B );              // makes local variable A a copy of B
```

In both instances of copying, a new class object is being created so a constructor must be called, called the **copy constructor**. If no copy constructor has been specified, the **default copy constructor** is used, which is a straight bit by bit copy.

To see why a copy constructor is needed, consider the following alteration to the stack generating program on p. 67. Here a `link1` object is passed by value.

```
#include "link1.h"

void aFun( link1 aLink ) // NOTE: value parameter
{
    ...
}

void main( void )
{
    list stack( -1.0 );       // list head

    stack.push( 1.1 );
    stack.push( 2.2 );
    stack.push( 3.3 ); // Now -1.0 ==> 3.3 ==> 2.2 ==> 1.1
```

```
aFun( stack );                  // how is stack copied??
    . . .
}
```

With no copy constructor, when `aFun` is called, the default copy constructor is called to create `aLink`, which gives the following situation:

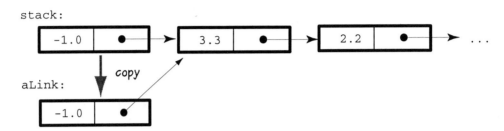

When `aFun` is exited, the destructor function is applied to `aLink`, with the following result (deleted memory shown grayed):

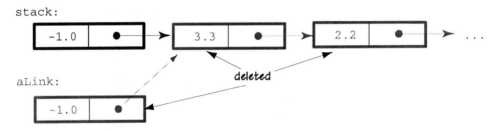

Now `stack.getLink()` points to memory that is no longer allocated — or worse, may be reallocated to something that isn't even a `link1`. The dreaded **dangling pointer** problem has occurred.

As with object deletion, we can solve the copy problem by defining a copy constructor explicitly.

> The general form of the copy constructor declaration is
> `classname ( classname & x )`. The parameter in the copy constructor *must* be passed by *reference*.

This isn't unreasonable since the copy constructor is *defining* how to pass a `classname` object by value!

For instance, a copy constructor for `link1` is declared as follows:

```
link1( link1 & aLink1 ); // copy constructor
```

An appropriate way to copy a linked list is to create a new list in newly allocated memory with copies of the `info` items. Thus we could define the copy constructor as follows:

```
link1::link1 ( link1 & aLink1 )
{
    link1 restoflist = aLink1.link ? new link1( *aLink1.link ) :
NULL;
                // call copy constructor recursively if necessary!!!!

    info = aLink1.info;       // this -> info = aLink1.info
    link = restoflist;    // this -> link = copy of rest of list
    }
}
```

Reconsidering the example at the beginning of this section, calling aFun creates the situation

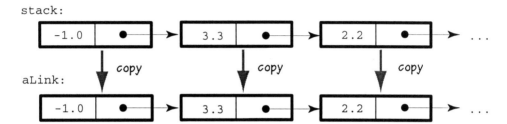

and after exiting aFun (and destroying aLink) we would have the safe situation

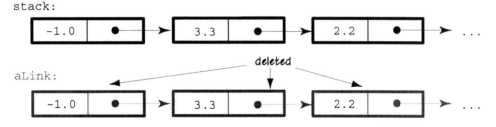

To summarize:

RULE

> Classes with data members that point to allocated memory should have explicit destructor and copy constructor functions.

In addition to the copy constructor, there is another copy operation for objects, operator= that is used for copying when the destination object already exists. For example

```
link1 a, b;
    ...
    a = b;   // uses operator=
```

As with other operators, the '=' operator can be overloaded. If operator= isn't given an explicit definition, it is also an exact copying operation. Note though that the specifications of operator= and the copy constructor are entirely independent. Either, neither, or both can be the default operation constructed by C++ when no explicit function is given. Note too the following:

```
link1 a, b = a;    // uses copy constructor to create b
  ...
   b = a;          // uses operator= to give b a value.
```

Exercises 8.3

1.   Write a member function to overload operator== for link1 objects. The operator should have the integer value 1 when applied to a pair of lists containing the same info data members, node for node, but need not have the same links. Otherwise the operator returns 0. (That is, a link1 object created by the copy constructor above will test equal to the object copied.)

2.   a)   Write a copy constructor for the btree class described in Exercise 8.1–1.

     b)   Once such a copy constructor exists, why is it even more important that the btree parameter to '<<' be passed by reference?

3.   If you wished to determine, by experiment, whether the copy constructor or operator= was called in the following declaration, how would you do it?

```
Date tomorrow = Date() + 1;
```

9. Hierarchies of Classes

The great power of computer programming is that it allows one to build complicated structures by pyramiding simple combinations of simple structures, level upon level. In ordinary programming this complexity is leveraged by ever greater levels of functions calling functions calling functions. Another way of handling complexity using Object-Oriented Programming is to build complex classes using hierarchies of simpler classes. In this chapter we will investigate some of the capabilities of C++ for doing this.

9.1 Derived Classes and Inheritance

Consider the following problem:

Normally, every item on a linked list has the same data type. This is because the 'next item' pointer has to be declared as a pointer to some fixed type. Suppose though that we wanted to have a list of objects of *different* types. Such a list is called a **polymorphic list** (*poly* = many, *morph* = form).

A good example of the desirability of polymorphic lists is found in programming a **windowing system**. If you have had much experience using computers, it is almost certain you have used such a system. For instance, a **window** is merely a rectangular area on the screen.

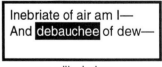
— the screen
— a window

Necessary data about a window would include where it is, how big it is, and what it contains. Various operations can be performed on a window, such as moving and resizing it. Since typically there may be several windows on the screen, this suggests that we declare a `class window` and that each particular window on the screen should be a `window` object. The use of OOP in general and C++ in particular has proven a very powerful tool in writing programs that manipulate windows.

a button

Two other objects of interest are the **button** and the **edit window,** each of which can be considered to be a special type of window. In addition, we can recognize a third type of window, the **dialog box**, which may contain one or more buttons and 0 or more editing windows!

Inebriate of air am I—
And debauchee of dew—

an edit window

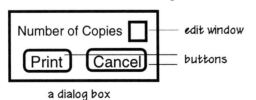
— edit window
— buttons

a dialog box

Thus, one of the pieces of data necessary to describe a dialog box is a list of various other windows objects it contains, i.e., a polymorphic list!

The contents of a dialog box are (generally) fixed. On the other hand, which windows are on the screen and their *stacking order* may vary widely with time. This requires another type of polymorphic list, a very volatile one.

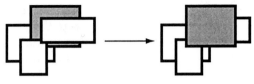

changing stacking order

On the left side of the diagram above, the shaded window is third from the front in the stacking order and to the right, it has been moved to the front (perhaps by clicking on it to make it the selected window). Of course, dialog boxes appear and disappear all the time.

At this point, you should be willing to accept the fact that polymorphic lists are very useful in implementing a windowing system. It is of course possible to create such lists in non-OOP languages.

To create polymorphic lists in C, we use `unions`. Looking at our example, we would of course have to declare our various data types as `struct`s:

polymorphic lists without C++

```
struct window { ... };
struct button { ... };
struct editWindow { ... };
struct dialogBox { ... };
```

Buttons, `editWindows`, and `dialogBoxes` are all special types of windows, so we would either have to repeat the `windows` data (such as location and size) or give each of these three `structs` a `window` substruct. The latter is a more structured approach, so we have in more detail

```
struct window {
   int xCoord, yCoord;    /* location of window */
   ...
};
struct button {
   struct window myWind;
   ...
};
struct editWindow {
   struct window myWind;
   etc.
```

An item for our polymorphic list can be declared

```
struct listItem {
   enum { aWindow, aButton, anEditWind, aDialogBox } whatAmI;
   union {    // contains exactly one of the following structs:
      struct window w;
      struct button b;
```

```
        struct editWindow e;
        struct dialogBox d;
    } any;
    struct listItem *next;
};
```

This is a mess, for several reasons:

problems with the C version

1. The particular type of object that the union contains can change, so C has to reserve enough storage for any one of the four possible objects. Thus storage can be wasted.

2. Something like the enum is necessary to be able to tell which type of object the union contains, and there is no protection against getting it wrong.

3. If p is a pointer to a listItem, *p always has an xCoord, but it must be obtained by different code depending on what object the union contains.

the same data item must be referenced in different ways

```
switch ( p -> whatAmI ) {
    case aWindow: x = (p -> any).w.xCoord; break;
    case aButton: x = (p -> any).b.myWind.xCoord; break;
    etc.
```

4. What if we add a new window type, such as an open file dialog? We must

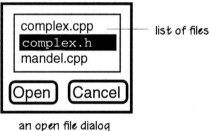

an open file dialog

obviously redefine the listItem struct to add an openFileDial, must recompile our *entire program*, and will probably have to rewrite many, if not all of the code pieces like that in reason 3. above. In addition, an openFileDial is a dialogBox, so its struct should contain a struct dialogBox myDial instead of a struct window myWind. Then the entry in the switch statement for an openFileDial above would be something like

```
case anOpenDialog:
    x = (p -> any).o.myDial.myWind.xCoord;...
```

5. Each of the five data types we have mentioned is in some sense a window. It would be nice to be able to write a function to process a generic window. The only way that could be done in C though would be to pass a structure like listItem (the next pointer field wouldn't be necessary, but everything else would be). Then once again, such a function would have to be rewritten if we added a new window type.

At this point, it should be clear that C isn't the solution. (Other non-OOP languages such as Pascal, Modula-2, and Ada have the same problems.) OOP to the rescue! The difference is that the older languages have only a HASA relationship:

```
struct blob {
```

```
   ...
   gloop x;        /* a blob HAS A gloop */
   ...
};
```

In C++ and other OOP languages, there is also an ISA relationship in data:

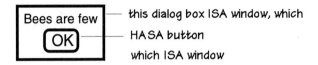

this dialog box ISA window, which

HASA button

which ISA window

The ISA relationship between classes is expressed in C++ as follows:

```
class gloop { ... } ;
class blob : public gloop
//  a blob     IS A   gloop
{ ... };
```

(Don't worry about the keyword `public`. Just use it.) In this situation we say that `gloop` is a **base class** and that `blob` is a **derived class** of the base class `gloop`, and **inherits** the properties (data and function elements) from `gloop`.

derived class ISA class

class HASA field

In the windowing example, we would declare

```
class window {
   int xCoord, yCoord;
   ...
};
class button : public window { ... }; // a button IS A window
class editWindow : public window { ... };
   // an editWindow IS A window
class dialogBox : public window { ... };
   // a dialogBox IS A window
class openFileDial : public dialogBox { ... };
   // an openFileDial IS A dialogBox, hence it also IS A window
```

None of the classes has any other explicit reference to `window`, but nonetheless contains ('is') one. In C++ terminology, `window` is the base class, and `button`, `editWindow`, and `dialogBox` are derived classes of that base class. In turn, `openFileDial` is a derived class of `dialogBox` (and `windows`).

If we declare

```
window *pw;
```

Then `pw` can point to a `window`, a `button`, an `editWindow`, a `dialogBox`, or an `openFileDial`, *or any other derived class of* `window` *that we might decide to define in the future,* and in *all* cases, we can set `x` to the `xCoord` of `*pw` with the statement

Important!

```
x = pw -> xCoord;
```

No code has to be rewritten or recompiled when a new class derived from the `window` class is defined, unless the code must deal explicitly with the newly defined derived class. `ListItem` is easily redeclared as:

```
struct listItem {
    window *pw;        // can point to a window or a button or ...
    struct listItem *next;
    };
```

and if as before, p is a `listItem *`, `p -> pw -> xCoord` is the x coordinate of the window. We can declare a function with a parameter of type `window` and pass to it an object of type `window`, `button`, `editWindow`, `dialogBox`, or `openFileDial`.

We can represent the hierarchical relationship of these classes as a tree:

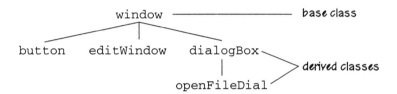

Descending lines connect a base class to classes derived from it. Each class lower down in the tree inherits all of the properties of the classes it descends from; that is, it has the data and function members of the class from which it is derived, plus other data and function members of its own.

9.2 Protected Class Members

Actually, inheritance is more complicated than we made it appear in the last section. The derived class inherits all members of its base class and can access the *public* members of the base class, but can not directly access private members. One could get around this by defining setters and accessers in the base class to handle the private members, but if these are visible in the derived class, they are visible everywhere. That could cause problems with data integrity. Therefore C++ has an intermediate mode of protection. Classes can declare **protected** members that are available to derived classes but not to the world at large. Protected members act just like public members in derived classes, and just like private members to the outside world.

In more detail, consider the following situation:

```
class B {   // B is the base class
    ...
    protected:
        int sortaSafe;
    ...
    sortaSafe cannot be accessed here as a member of a DB object!
    };
```

```
class DB: public B {      // DB is a class derived from B
{
```

*sortaSafe acts like a public data member of DB inside
here and also inside the definition of any DB member function.*

sortaSafe is a private member of any B object here and cannot be accessed!

```
};
```

*Outside of the class declarations of B and DB, and the definitions
of any of their member functions,* sortaSafe *is private and cannot
be accessed at all.*

Consider the following example to show how protected data members might be used:

Suppose that we want to set up various types of bank accounts. All of these accounts will have certain pieces of information in common, such as the name and address of the account holder, so we will define a base account class to include this data. The various types of accounts — loan, savings, etc. — will each constitute a class derived from the account class.

Each account will also have a *balance*. The various derived classes will have to manipulate the balance in different ways, but integrity of the balance must be maintained, so we will make the balance a protected member of the account class:

```
class account { // the base class
   // account-holder information
   protected:
      double balance;
   ...
};
```

A class for savings accounts could be declared as follows (all functions are shown inline for simplicity, but they could also be declared here and defined elsewhere):

```
class savings: public account {
   ...
   public:
      void deposit( double amt ) { balance += amt; }
      double withdraw( double amt ) {
         if ( amt <= balance ) {
            balance -= amt;
            return amt;
            }
         else return 0;
      }
   ...
};
```

A loan class would be somewhat different:

```
class loan: public account {
    ...
  public:
    void payment( double amt )
        { balance -= amt - accrued interest; }
    ...
};
```

Suppose we try to define a `transfer` function in the loan class to transfer an amount from another account to the current one. The following won't work:

```
class loan: public account {
    ...
    void transfer( double amt, account act ) {
        balance -= amt - accrued interest;
        act.balance -= amt;    // illegal; act isn't a loan object
    }
};
```

To emphasize the reason, we give the following rule:

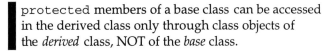 `protected` members of a base class can be accessed in the derived class only through class objects of the *derived* class, NOT of the *base* class.

(We could use the always popular and dangerous type cast to coerce `act` to be a `loan` object. For more on this approach, see Chapter 10, p. 104)

Exercises 9.2

1. Add the data members `double interestRate` and `Date lastPayment` to the `loan` class. Rewrite the payment function so that it uses these variables to actually compute accrued interest, and then updates `lastPayment` with today's date. (Assume that every year has 365 days for simplicity.)

2. Declare a `checking` class that is similar to the savings class except that it includes a data member `double bounceFee` that is deducted from the balance whenever there is not enough money in the account for a requested withdrawal.

9.3 Constructors and Destructors

Constructors and destructors aren't exactly inherited by derived classes. Consider the following situation:

```
class B{ ... };                   // Base class

class DB: public B { ... };       // Derived class

class DDB: public DB {            // Derived from derived class
    ...
    DDB( ... parameters ... )     // a particular constructor for DDB
```

```
      . . .
   };
```

When the given constructor for DDB is executed, the standard behavior is that C++ first automatically executes the *default* constructors for B and DB, in that order, then the specified constructor for DDB. When a DDB object is destroyed, the destructors are called in reverse order: ~DDB(), ~DB(), and finally ~B().

This behavior is usually sufficient for destructors since they have no parameters, but this arrangement of constructors leaves something to be desired. In the window example, when we create a dialogBox, we need to specify its basic window properties, such as its location and size. Default values simply won't do — for instance, we would certainly want different default values than for buttons. We can in fact override the default behavior and precisely specify the order in which constructors are executed with a definition of the DDB constructor like

explicitly specifying constructors for derived classes

```
DDB( ... parameters ... ) : constructor1, constructor2, ...
      // here put ';' if constructor is defined elsewhere or
      // { inline definition }
```

The constructors are executed in the order *constructor1*, *constructor2*, ..., and then DDB(...) itself. The list of parameters to DDB can include parameters that are passed explicitly to *constructor1*, *constructor2*, ... For instance in the window example we could declare

```
dialogBox::dialogBox( int xPos, int yPos, ... )
      : window( xPos, yPos, ...);
{ /* separate definition in .cpp file */ }
```

Exercise 9.3

1.   Define a constructor function for the class loan described in section 9.2 and Exercise 9.2–1. The constructor is to have three parameters, loanAmount, InterestRate, and loanStartDate, the last defaulting to today's date.

9.4.   Virtual Functions

There is one more question to be answered before we can make practical use of derived classes. When we have declared window *pw, then pw can point to a class object of window or any of the four classes derived from it. Any member data or function of the base window class can be accessed through pw in the same way no matter what pw is pointing to. But we may also want to treat the window differently depending on what kind it is.

Suppose for instance that we have a list of window objects and we want to display each object on the screen. In the C method we had an enum whatAmI that told us the type of object in the union. We could do that in C++, but there is a much better way. In the case at hand, each class needs a member function to display its objects. This suggests something like an overloaded function, called say showMe(), in each class to do the displaying. If we try to do this with ordinary overloaded functions, it doesn't work:

```
void ShowMe( window W ) ...
void ShowMe( button B ) ...

button OKButton;
window *pw = &OKButton;
   ...
   showMe( OKButton );     // invokes the button showMe function
   ...
   showMe( *pw );          // invokes the window showMe function!!!
```

The problem is that the compiler cannot know what pw is going to be pointing to at run time, and it can be pointing to a different type of window each time the statement is executed.

C++ gets around this problem with another sort of overloading, the **virtual function**. Virtual functions can only be declared as class member functions. A function is declared virtual by placing the keyword virtual ahead of the ordinary function declaration in the base class. Unlike overloaded functions, whose declarations must all be different, the declarations of virtual functions must all be the same! The 'overloading' is sorted out by the implicit parameter this passed to all member functions.

virtual functions figure out which version to run by looking at which class an object is in at runtime

If we have declared

```
class B {   // the base class
   ...
   virtual void vf( ... );
};

class DB { // class derived from B
   ...
};

class DDB {   // class derived from DB
   ...
};

B *pB;   // pB can point to a B, a DB, or a DDB
```

and we evaluate pB -> vf(...), C++ will check the type of *pB *at runtime*. If *pB is a DDB object, a DDB version of vf is executed, if one exists. If not, we search up the tree, in this case, first DB then B until a function vf is found, and that function is executed.

In the window example, we would declare

```
class window {
   ...
   virtual void showMe( void );
};
class button : public window {
   ...
   void showMe( void );     // keyword virtual optional here
};
```

```
button OKButton;
window *pw = OKButton;
   ...
   showMe( OKButton );     // invokes the button showMe function
   ...
   showMe( *pw );          // also invokes button showMe function!!!
```

Compared to overloaded functions, the power of virtual functions is not achieved without a cost.

First of all, when a member function is declared virtual, every object of the class and of every derived class must have a 'secret' data member telling which class it is, so the appropriate virtual function can be selected. That is, each class has a secret whoAmI data member.

Secondly, the correct choice of overloaded function can always be determined at compile time. For virtual functions, each time such a function is invoked a run-time search must be performed, starting at the class of the object and working up the tree until a virtual function is found. Thus there is both a space penalty and a time penalty for virtual functions.

Exercises 9.4

1.   Suppose we declare

```
class A {
     ...
   public:
     ...
   virtual void who ( void ) { cout << "A object "; }
};

class B: public A {
     ...
   public:
     ...
   void who ( void ) { cout << "B object "; }
};

class C: public B {
     ...
   public:
     ...

     void who( void ) { cout << "C object "; }
};

A *p1, *p2, *p3;    // all pointers of type A *, but can
                    //  also point to a B or a C.
```

a)   What will be displayed by the code

```
p1 = new A; p2 = new B; p3 = new C;
p1 -> who(); p2 -> who(); p3 -> who(); cout << endl;
```

b)   Given the code above, what will be displayed by the code

```
((B *)p3) -> who();
```

2.   Show how to declare a virtual function WhoAmI in the five windows classes such that pw -> WhoAmI() returns enum values aWindow if pw happens to be pointing to a window, aButton if pw is pointing to a button, etc.

3.   Is it possible to have an overloaded virtual function? (Experimentation is probably necessary.)

10. Discrete System Simulation

Classes were originally invented as a mechanism in the discrete system simulation language Simula 67. In this section, we will attempt to give the flavor of classes and Object-Oriented Programming used in simulation.

This type of simulation is called **discrete** because the movement of time will be simulated in discrete jumps, rather than continuously. The objects of our simulation may be people or machines or highways or cars. Each object will follow its own plan, which I call its **script**. Each object in the simulation is scheduled to perform a particular action from its script, called a **scene**, at some particular time. It is also possible though that the object might be waiting for something to occur not directly tied to time — usually, for some resource to become available.

An object scheduled to perform a particular scene at a particular time is called an **event**. A simulation program will be controlled by an **event queue**, which is a list of events ordered by the time they are to occur. A typical simulation will involve objects of different types, so the event queue will be a *polymorphic list*, as discussed in section 9.1.

The main loop of our simulation program is incredibly simple as all the work has been pushed down into the classes:

the fundamental loop

```
while ( more events in the queue ) {
    remove first ( = earliest ) event from the queue ;
    set 'now' = eventTime of this event
    perform the scene specified for the event ;
}
```

The variable now is kept as a simulation of the current time. From an object's point of view, it is waiting to perform an action. When the time for the action comes, the action is performed, after which the object specifies the time and action it wants to perform next and goes back to waiting. As with the object-oriented example in Chapter 6, each individual action is often quite simple to program, and can be composed largely independently of all the other actions.

The result of this technique is that complicated situations involving many actions happening continuously and simultaneously are simulated by objects executing sequentially and in discrete jumps of time. By making the time steps small enough, the original problem with continuous time and actions occurring in parallel can be represented quite realistically. (This is the way a time-shared operating system simulates many simultaneously executing programs when it can actually execute only one at a time.)

To give you an idea of what is going on, let's develop some scenes for a script for a family getting up in the morning. A family consists of a group of persons and persons have many traits in common, so this suggests a class person and one class object representing each member of the family. Differences in roles, requirements, etc., will be expressed by different values of data members.

The event of waking up in the morning is a useful example. First of all, its time can be determined in three ways: 1) by the setting of an alarm to a particular time,

2) by being awakened by some other family member, or 3) by just waking up when you feel like it. Since class objects can't feel, we simulate 3) by choosing the wakeup time randomly, based perhaps on personal characteristics expressed by the data members. Method 2) can be handled by giving each person a (possibly empty) list of persons he or she is to wake up. Thus at the start of our day simulation, each person will be on exactly one list: the event queue, with a specific wakeup time, or the wakeup list of some other person (who could also be on someone else's wakeup list). Finally, to add further to the reality, we could allow some people to go back to sleep for a certain amount of time, which we will also determine randomly based on data members.

Let's look at the wake-up scene as we have it so far. We'll give the scenes descriptive names, which we will show with <u>double underlining</u>.

```
// person script (fragment)
wake up :
        Determine 'moreTime' = amount of more sleep I want (random
            number generator)
        if ( moreTime > 0 ) Schedule me ( = *this ) for wakeup at
            now + moreTime and go back to sleep
        while ( list of people to wake up is non-empty )
          remove first person from the list and Schedule her to
            wake up now (i.e., after I finish executing)
        Schedule next event: 'wash up' for a certain amount of
            time
```

The final event of this scene is interesting. Suppose that persons may only use a bathroom one at a time. We will create a bathroom class with one object per actual bathroom to handle this. Normally a bathroom will be unoccupied with no one waiting, which will be indicated by its being on no list. In such a state, the bathroom too will have a wakeup event, when someone wants to use it. The script for a bathroom might be

```
// bathroom script (complete)
wake up :
        If someone is waiting on my list, take the first person
            off waiting list and schedule him or her how.
        go back to sleep
```

We can now add more detail to the person script:

```
// person script (fragment)
wake up :
            ...
          // after waking up other people:
        Determine 'washUpTime' and bathroom based on my habits
            (more data elements)
        Put me on the list waiting for the particular bathroom
            with 'wash up' as my next event; If bathroom is
            'asleep', schedule a wakeup event for it now (just
            after this event finishes)
```

<u>wash up</u> :

```
        Schedule me for 'eat breakfast' at now + washUpTime.
        Schedule the bathroom for a wakeup event at now +
            washUpTime.
```
<u>eat breakfast</u> :

```
        ...
```

Randomness as we have used it here is very important in simulation. Suppose we are simulating a highway where cars enter the highway on the average of one per minute and travel at an average of 53 miles per hour. The road might seem to operate quite well under the assumption that cars arrived exactly a minute apart and all go exactly 53 miles per hour, whereas the clumping that happens in real life might cause horrendous traffic jams.

Now let's talk about some more details of implementation. As we have seen, the objects of our simulation will be class objects of various classes. All of the objects have certain properties and functions in common, such as scheduling functions and event times. In addition, each class will have a script function, though different classes will have different scripts. This suggests a common base class for all objects of simulation, which I will call the process class. This base class will contain all the common functions and data and will declare a virtual function script() (see section 9.4). Each process object will have a variable telling it what scene it is to execute next, so different objects of the same class can be executing different scenes 'simultaneously'.

script is a virtual function

A preliminary form of the declarations is

```
double now;                    // current time

class process {
   protected:
      double eventTime;       // time the event is to occur
      int nextScene;          // next scene to be executed
      ...
   virtual void script( void ) { }     // never called
};

class person : public process {
   ...
   enum { wakeUp, washUp, eatBreakfast, ... };
      // give symbolic names to the numbers
      // used for nextScene. This is OK since C and C++
      // don't distinguish between enums and ints.
   void script( void ) {
      switch( nextScene ) {
         wakeUp:
      ...
};

class bathroom : public process {
   ...
   void script( void ) { // only scene is wakeUp
      ...
};
```

As it turns out, we will actually use a three-tiered structure because certain features of processes turn out to be useful in other objects as well. As we have seen, we have objects in lists dependent on time and objects in lists not dependent on time. This suggests an even more basic class than `process`, a class of linked-list nodes. Since in the event queue we have to insert processes randomly according to their time of occurrence, we will base `process` on a new class `link2` of nodes in a *doubly* linked list. Thus our final structure of derived classes will be

```
class link2 {
   ...
   link2 *next, *prev;   // forward and backward links
   ...
};

class process : public link2 {
   ...
};

class person : public process {
   ...
};
etc.
```

We can picture some of the class objects as follows:

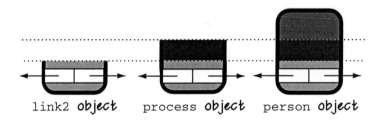

link2 *object*   process *object*   person *object*

Let's start building up our infrastructure. Points of interest are shown in **boldface**.

```
// link2.h -- base class for doubly linked lists

#include <stdlib.h>

int counter;  // supplies unique ID number for each link2 object

class link2 {
   protected:
      link2 *next, *prev;   // can also point to a process, etc.
      int id;

   public:
      // constructor
      link2( link2 *np = NULL, link2 *pp = NULL )
         { next = np;  prev = pp;  id = ++counter; }
```

```
    // destructor
     ~link2( void ) { Unlink(); }     // don't leave pointers
            //  to *this lying about

    // accessers
     link2 *getNext( void ) { return next; }
     link2 *getPrev( void ) { return prev; }
     int getId( void ) { return id; }

    // setters
     void After( link2 & L ); // insert *this after L
     void Before( link2 & L );        // insert *this before L
     void Unlink( void );     // unlink *this from whatever
        // list it might be currently in

     virtual void print( void );
        // print identifying message for debugging
};
```

A link2 object is mostly standard stuff, having pointers to its successor and predecessor in the list and containing a unique ID number that can be used for debugging purposes. In addition, we have a virtual function print() which will display that number and the node type, as well as other helpful information.

The definition of print() in link2.cpp is

```
#include <iostream.h>

void link2::print( void )
{
   cout << "link2[" << id << "]";
}
```

The definitions of the remaining member functions of the link2 class are straightforward exercises in manipulating doubly linked lists.

```
void link2::Unlink( void )
{
   if ( next != NULL ) {
      next -> prev = prev;
      prev -> next = next;
      }
   next = prev = NULL;
}


void link::Before( link2 & L ) // L.prev ==> this ==> L
{
   if ( this == &L ) return;  // nothing required to link this
                              // before itself
   Unlink();

   next = &L;
   prev = L.prev;
   L.prev -> next = this;
```

```
        L.prev = this;
    }
    void link2::After(... // very similar to Before
```

You can see the effect of these procedures by drawing diagrams and following the arrows. As an example, the following is the situation before Before is executed:

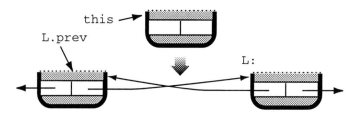

insert *this
Before L

As a result of executing Before, we have

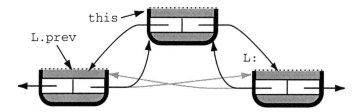

Our lists will be headed by a special link2 object called a queue object so that just as with stacks in section 8.1, there will always be something there even when the list is empty. The successor to the last item on the list will be the queue object and the predecessor of the queue object will be the last list item. The queue class is declared as follows:

```
// queue.h -- a queue structure for links

#include "link2.h"

class queue: public link2 {
    public:
        // constructor
        queue( void ) : link2( this, this ) { }

        // destructor
        ~queue( void );

        int isEmpty( void ) { return next == this; }
        void addLast ( link2 & L ) { L.Before( *this ) ; }
        link2 & getFirst( void );

        virtual void print( void );
};
```

Note that the constructor for a queue explicitly invokes the link2 constructor (see section 9.3) to create an empty queue as follows:

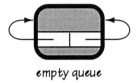

empty queue

Note that a new item is added to the end of a queue by linking it in *before* the queue object. If we execute the following code

```
queue q;

queue.addLast( * new queue);
queue.addLast( * new queue);
queue.addLast( * new queue);
```

the queue object would look as follows:

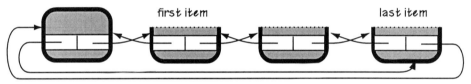

queue with three items

The code necessary to implement the member functions which aren't inline is

```
// queue.cpp -- code for queue class

#include <iostream.h>
#include <assert.h>
#include "queue.h"

queue::~queue( void )     // destructor function
{
   while ( ! isEmpty() )     // delete queue header and
      delete & getFirst( ); //  everything on the queue

   next = prev = NULL;
}

link2 & queue::getFirst( void )
{
   link2 *pL;

   assert( ! isEmpty( ) );

   pL = next;
   pL -> Unlink( );
   return *pL;
```

```
        }

        void queue::print( void )   // display whole queue
        {
           cout << "queue[" << id << "]: ";

           for ( link2 *pL = next; pL != this; pL = pL -> getNext( ) ) {
              pL -> print( );
              cout << " ";
              }
           cout << endl;
        }
```

If we create the `queue` object `q` as we did above containing three items and then execute the statement

```
        q.print();
```

the resulting output is

```
        queue[1]: link2[2] link2[3] link2[4]
```

In the `for` loop in `queue::print` there is the statement `pL = pL -> getNext()`. You may have wondered why we didn't just say `pL = pL.next` since we are in a class derived from the `link2` class and `next` is a protected member of the `link2` class. To answer this question, refer to the rule on p. 81. Inside a class, we can refer to protected members of the class only through objects *of that class itself*, not through objects of the base class. That is, if we are inside `queue` and declare

```
        link2 L, *pL;
        queue Q, *pQ;
```

then

>   `L.next` and `pL -> next` are ILLEGAL
>   because we are *outside* `link2` and trying to access protected members of `link2`.
>   `Q.next` and `pQ -> next` are LEGAL
>   because we are *inside* `queue` accessing protected members of its base class.

We could have gotten around this by using `((queue *)pL) -> next` but I think this is dangerous since *none* of the items on the list are actually `queue` items.

Now let's develop the `process` class.

```
        // process.h -- class for elementary discrete system simulation

        #include "queue.h"
```

```
extern queue *eventqueue;
extern double now; // time of first process on eventqueue
   // = eventqueue -> next -> eventTime

class process: public link2 {
   protected:
      double eventTime;      // time the event is to occur
      int nextScene;         // next scene to be executed

   public:
      // constructors
      process( double occursAt ) { Schedule( occursAt ); }
      process( void ) { /* doesn't schedule process */ }

      // accesser
      double occurs( void ) { return eventTime; }

      void Schedule( double at, int scene = 0 );
      void Delay( double interval, int scene = -1 )
         // can't say int scene = nextScene+1 because for all
         // C++ knows, Delay could be called outside a process,
         // where nextScene won't be available
         { Schedule( now + interval,
               (scene >= 0) ? scene : (nextScene + 1) ); }
      void Terminate( void ) { Unlink( ); delete this; }

      virtual void script( void ) {} // never called
};

void nextEvent( void );    // finds next event in the eventqueue
   // and executes the nextScene of its script.
```

Notice that we have included two different types of process scheduling: Schedule, which schedules an event at an absolute time, and Delay that schedules an event for some given amount of time after now. For Schedule, the default scene is 0, which is always the starting scene, and for Delay, it is the next scene, nextScene (= current scene + 1).

Note that eventqueue isn't really a queue, since events don't have to enter the queue at the end. They do leave from the front, though. (eventqueue is actually a *priority queue*.)

The definitions are straightforward. Schedule works by doing an insertion sort starting at the end of eventqueue and working forward until the proper place is found.

```
// process.cpp -- code for process class

#include <assert.h>
#include <iostream.h>
#include "process.h"

double now = 0;
queue *eventqueue = new queue;
```

```
void process::Schedule( double at, int scene )
{
    assert( at >= now );

    eventTime = at;
    link2 *p = eventqueue -> getPrev(); // p --> end of queue
    while ( p != eventqueue && eventTime <
                                ((process *)p) -> eventTime )
        p = p -> getPrev();
    After( *p );
    nextScene = scene;
}

void nextEvent( void )
{
    if ( eventqueue -> isEmpty() ) {   // is there an event?
        cout << "no event to schedule; terminating program" <<
               endl;
        exit( 1 );
        }
    process *p = (process *)(eventqueue -> getNext());
    now = p -> occurs( ); // p --> first event
    p -> script();   // execute the next scene of the first event
}
```

Now that we have developed all the machinery we need for simulation, it is time to give some examples. For our first example, we will solve a problem which at first glance doesn't seem like a simulation problem at all. Our solution will be in some respects more complicated than the usual methods not involving simulation.

Example 10.1: The **sieve of Eratosthenes** is a method of finding all prime numbers less than a given number.[8] To perform this method by hand, you write out all the numbers from 2 to your upper limit. Circle 2 and cross out all the multiples of 2. Find the first uncrossed and uncircled number (in this case 3), circle it, and cross out all its multiples. Repeat the last sentence until all numbers are crossed out or circled. The circled numbers are the primes. For instance in the following list,

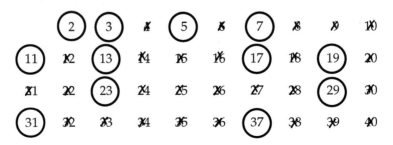

---

[8]A number is **prime** if it is divisible only by itself and 1. 1 itself is usually not considered a prime. The first few primes are 2, 3, 5, 7, 11, 13, 17, ….

we first circled 2 and crossed out all other even numbers. Then 3 was circled and we crossed out 9, 15, 21, 27, 33, and 39, which hadn't been previously crossed out. 5 was circled and we crossed out 25 and 35. All remaining uncrossed numbers have no new multiples within the range shown, so all remaining uncrossed numbers are primes.

In attempting to program this method, it is first evident that we can make our list half as long by writing down only the odd numbers and treating 2 as a special case. We only have to cross out odd multiples of primes, too, since the even ones are already gone.

Simulation enters the picture as follows. The event times will either be a number to be circled or a number to be crossed out (erased). The two scenes will be 'cross out this number' and 'circle this number'. The main object of our simulation will be of a `class prime: public process` with a data member `thePrime` and the following script:

<u>circle prime</u>
     do the circling and execute 'cross out multiple' below
<u>erase multiple</u>
     if there is no event at now + 2, that number is a new prime so generate a new prime object scheduled at now + 2 with nextScene equal to 'circle prime'.
     In any case, reschedule this object to erase the next multiple of thePrime.

The mechanism for circling the prime will just be to output the prime as part of a comma-separated list of primes. The cross-out method is a **lazy evaluation**: instead of erasing all the multiples of `thePrime`, we schedule erasing the next multiple and when we get to it, schedule the erasing of another. Rescheduling for the next erasure is just `Delay( 2*thePrime )`. Thus we can add detail to our script as follows:

<u>circle prime</u>
     cout << thePrime << ", " and fall through to
<u>erase multiple</u>
     if (next -> eventTime > now + 2)
      new prime with eventTime = thePrime = now+2 and nextScene equal to 'circle prime'.
     Delay(2 * thePrime, 'erase multiple')

The declaration for `prime` is

```
#include "process.h"
#include "strlen.h"   // overloaded strlen function from Ex 4.3—1

class prime: public process {
  private:
    int thePrime;
    enum { circlePrime, eraseMultiple };   // = 0, 1

  public:
```

```
                    // constructor
                    prime( double p ) : process( p ) { thePrime = (int)p; }
                        // p actually equals my eventTime

            void script( void );
            void print( void );
        };

        int outcol     // running total of number of cols of output on
                        // current line.
        #define LINEWIDTH 66      // number of columns in a line

        void prime::script( void )
        {
            int len;

            switch ( nextScene ) {
            case circlePrime:
                len = strlen( thePrime );
                    // overloaded version from Ex 3.3-2 a)
                outcol += len;
                if ( outcol >= LINEWIDTH-2 ) { // avoid running off end
                    cout << endl;
                    outcol = len;
                    }
                outcol += 2;
                cout << thePrime << ", ";       // then, fall through to
            case eraseMultiple:
                if ( eventTime + 2 < ((prime *)next) -> eventTime )
                    // must cast to prime to use protected variable
                    //  eventTime. ((process *) won't work
                    //  see rule on p. 81
                    new prime( eventTime + 2 );
                Delay( 2 * thePrime, eraseMultiple );
            }
        }

        void prime::print( void )
        {
            cout << "prime[" << id << "] is " << thePrime << " at time "
                << eventTime << endl;
        }
```

In order to keep our prime display from straddling lines, we have kept a count of the number of columns on the current line, using the overloaded `strlen` function developed in Exercise 3.3–2 a.

In order to stop this program, we need a second type of process, a `stopper` process that will sit on the event queue and terminate the program when we get to it. It is defined by

```
enum { FALSE, TRUE }; // = 0, 1 respectively
int running;     // used to terminate nextEvent() loop

class stopper: public process {
```

```
   public:
     // Constructor
     stopper( double largestPrime ) : process( largestPrime ) {
}

     void script( void );
     void print( void );
};

void stopper::script( void )
{     // only one scene
   cout << "..." << endl << "Done" << endl;
   running = FALSE;    // exit nextEvent() loop
}

void stopper::print( void )
{
   cout << "stopper[" << id << "] at time " << eventTime << endl;
}
```

We have now done all the work, and the rest of the program is simple:

```
// sieve.cpp--finds number of primes less than some number
//          using the sieve of Eratosthenes

#include "process.h"
#include <iostream.h>
#include "strlen.h"

   { class stopper definitions }
   { class prime definitions }

void main( void )
{
   new stopper( 500 );
   new prime( 3 );  // give eventqueue a prime to process

   cout << "2, ";   // treat 2 specially
   outcol = 3;

   running = TRUE;
   while ( running )
      nextEvent();  // all the work happens here!!
}
```

the fundamental
loop

The result of executing the program is

```
2, 3, 5, 7, 11, 13, 17, 19, 23, 29, 31, 37, 41, 43, 47, 53, 59,
61, 67, 71, 73, 79, 83, 89, 97, 101, 103, 107, 109, 113, 127,
131, 137, 139, 149, 151, 157, 163, 167, 173, 179, 181, 191, 193,
197, 199, 211, 223, 227, 229, 233, 239, 241, 251, 257, 263, 269,
271, 277, 281, 283, 293, 307, 311, 313, 317, 331, 337, 347, 349,
353, 359, 367, 373, 379, 383, 389, 397, 401, 409, 419, 421, 431,
433, 439, 443, 449, 457, 461, 463, 467, 479, 487, 491, 499, ...
Done
```

When now = 9.0, the event queue appears as follows:

Executing the event at time 9.0 will cause a new prime object to be created for the prime 11 and the prime 3 will be delayed 2 * 3, that is, it will be rescheduled at 15.0:

Example 10.2: We have finally developed enough machinery that we can easily program a simple simulation. The problem is to simulate a **single server queue**. This is a situation where customers arrive at random times and are to be served by a single clerk, called the **server**, who takes random amounts of time to serve them. If the clerk is free when the customer arrives, service takes place immediately. Otherwise, the customer waits in a queue and waiting customers are served on a first come-first served basis.

For our problem, we will have two types of objects, customer objects and a clerk object. As before, we will have a stopper object to put a time limit on the simulation.

A simple-minded version of the clerk script might be as follows:

```
Start Processing Customer        // FLAWED!!
        Take first customer from waiting line and remember its
            arrival time;
        Generate random service time and Delay( service time,
            Finish Processing Customer);
Finish Processing Customer
          Record statistics for customer and go to Start Processing
            Customer.
```

The problem is that there may be no customers waiting in line. This is the same kind of problem we ran into with the bathroom process. We have to put the clerk (or bathroom) to sleep, and handling a sleeping process is a slightly tricky problem. The process can't wake itself up since it doesn't know when that is going to happen. It could reinsert itself in the event queue at periodic intervals and check, but this costs program time and simulated real time.[9] As before, we solve the problem by having the customer wake up the clerk when it arrives in the system (if

[9]If this discussion reminds you of problems of operating systems and polling versus interrupt-driven operations, you are precisely correct.

the clerk is asleep). This will mean scheduling the clerk "right now". The script for the customer is

<u>arrive</u>
```
    generate arrival event for next customer
    add me to the end of the waiting line
    if clerk is asleep, wake him up by scheduling him now.
```

and the altered `clerk` script is

<u>Wake Up</u>
```
        If the waiting line is empty, go to sleep, i.e., remove
            myself from the eventqueue and set nextScene to Wake
            Up.
        Take first customer from waiting line and remember its
            arrival time;
        Generate random service time and Delay( service time,
            Finish Processing Customer);
```
<u>Finish Processing Customer</u>
```
        Record statistics for customer and go to Wake Up.
```

random numbers and their distributions

The only thing left to do in constructing the program is to decide how to generate the random arrival and service times. Notice that we used a lazy method of generating customers, with each customer generating the next customer. It turns out that an **exponential distribution** of arrivals and service times is often a reasonable model of the real world.[10] With an exponential distribution, we will generate positive random numbers that can be arbitrarily large. The average value generated will be finite and the higher numbers are less likely to appear.

We will start construction of our random numbers from the standard UNIX C random number generating function `int rand( void )` which returns a uniformly distributed random number between 0 and RAND_MAX (inclusive).[11] (RAND_MAX and the prototype for `rand` are defined in `stdlib.h`.) First, we need a more standard version of `rand()`, one that returns a `double` x satisfying $0 \leq x < 1$. That we can do as follows:

```
double random( void ) // 0 <= random() < 1
{
    return rand( )/(1.0 + RAND_MAX);
}
```

We add 1 to the denominator so that `random` doesn't assume the value 1, and 1.0 is used to force the denominator to type `double` so that `double` (not `int`) division is performed. (RAND_MAX is probably also the largest positive integer, so

---

[10]See just about any book on probability for a discussion of exponential distributions. For example, see K. L. Chung, *Elementary Probability Theory with Stochastic Processes*, Springer-Verlag, 1974, p. 98.

[11]Uniform distribution means that each value occurs about equally often.

1+RAND_MAX is probably negative!) An exponentially distributed random number is then generated as follows[12]

```
double expRand( double mean )
              // returns exponentially distributed
{             // pseudo-random numbers with mean 'mean'
   return -log(1 - random( )) * mean;
}
```

We can make up header and definition files as follows:

```
// random.h--random number generators

extern double random( void );
extern double expRand( double mean );
```

and

```
// random.cpp--definitions of random number generators

#include <stdlib.h>   // for rand() declarations
#include <math.h>     // for log () function
#include "random.h"

double random( void )
   ...
double expRand( double mean )
   ...
```

At this point it is easy to construct the classes. The class declarations are as follows

```
enum { FALSE, TRUE }; // FALSE = 0, TRUE = 1

class customer: public process {
   private:
      double arrivalTime;

   public:
     // constructor
      customer( double arTime ) : process( arTime )
        { arrivalTime = arTime; }

     // accesser
      double arriveTime( void ) { return arrivalTime; }

   void script( void );
   void print( void );
};
```

---

[12]The only reference in print I know of which derives this is my book *Programming Concepts, A Second Course* (Prentice-Hall, 1982), pp. 212-214, which unfortunately is out of print.

```
class clerk: public process {
  private:
    int asleep;
    enum { wakeUp, finishService }; // scenes
    double customerArrivalTime;

  public:
    // constructor
    clerk( void ) : process( void ) { asleep = TRUE; }

    // accesser
    int isAsleep( void ) { return asleep; }

  void script( void );
  void print( void );
};
```

Note that by invoking process() in the clerk constructor, we don't schedule the clerk initially. (C++ would automatically call process() if no initialization were specified, but I feel it is safer to do it explicitly.) Next we define the globals:

```
int customerCount = 0;
double timeWaitingInQueue = 0.0;
double totalWaitingTime = 0.0;

double meanArrivalTime = 5.0;  // for the purpose of example
double meanServiceTime = 4.0;

clerk theClerk;
queue waitQueue;    // waiting line
```

The customer script is then straightforward:

```
void customer::script( void )
{
  ++ customerCount;  // count customer
  // then generate the next one
  new customer( now + expRand( meanArrivalTime ));
  waitQueue.addLast( *this ); // stand at the end of the line
  if ( theClerk.isAsleep( ) )
    theClerk.Schedule( now );      // wake up clerk
}
```

Notice how naturally the customer code can be written. The code for clerks is a little more unpleasant:

```
void clerk::script( void )
{
  switch ( nextScene ) {
  case finishService: // scene 1
    totalWaitingTime += now - customerArrivalTime;
        // now perform wakeup actions
  case wakeUp:         // scene 0
```

```
        if ( waitQueue.isEmpty( ) ) {   // go to sleep
          asleep = TRUE;
          nextScene = wakeUp;
          Unlink( );
          return;
          }
        asleep = FALSE;
        customerArrivalTime =
          ((customer *)waitQueue.Next()) -> arriveTime( );
        timeWaitingInQueue += now - customerArrivalTime;
        ((customer &)(waitQueue.getFirst())).Terminate() ;
        Delay( expRand( meanServiceTime ), finishService );
      }
    }
```

Notice the boldface expressions. One of the stated design criteria for C++ was to protect the programmer by doing more type checking than C. Unfortunately, it often seems that one has to come up with ghastly expressions like these which disable the checking mechanism in order to get anything done. (This is the rule from p. 81 again.)

Finally, the stopper class is declared as in the sieve program and has the following script:

```
int running;  // used to stop nextEvent() loop

void stopper::script( void )
{
    cout << "Customers served: " << customerCount << endl;
    cout << "Average wait time until service: " <<
        timeWaitingInQueue / customerCount << endl;
    cout << "Average total waiting time: " <<
        totalWaitingTime / customerCount << endl;
    cout << "Expected average total waiting time: " <<
        1/(1/meanServiceTime - 1/meanArrivalTime) << endl;
    running = FALSE;
}
```

The last line of output is based on the fact that in a single-server queue, if arrivals are exponentially distributed with mean A and service times are exponentially distributed with mean S and the system runs long enough to achieve equilibrium, the expected total waiting time for each customer is $1/(1/A - 1/S)$.

The print functions for the three classes are routine, so we only need to give the main program:

```
void main( void )
{
    new stopper ( 30000 );
    new customer ( 0.0 );

    running = TRUE;
    while ( running )
        nextEvent();
}
```

the fundamental
loop, yet again

A time limit of 30000 seemed necessary to reach equilibrium with our chosen means. The output of the program was

```
Customers served:6032
Average wait time until service: 15.622349
Average total waiting time: 19.624568
Expected average total waiting time: 20
```

Note that at the end of the simulation, we may have processed only part of a customer, so the results may be slightly skewed. When spread over 6000 customers though, this should be insignificant. One method of avoiding this (slight) problem is given in Exercise 10–5c below.

Exercises 10

1. Note that in process::Schedule we could also have said 'eventqueue -> prev', but not 'p -> prev'. Why?

2. The parameters to Before and After *must* be reference types. Why?

3. When the sieve program is done, there will be a number of prime objects on the eventqueue that are never used since they follow the stopper object. Rewrite the script for prime objects so that they get Terminated rather than being put on the queue after the stopper.

4. Why can't the print virtual function be an overload of the << operator?

5. This exercise suggests various modifications to ssqueue.cpp, the single-server queue example:

    a) Add a facility to the queue class that keeps track of the number of items in the queue, exclusive of the header, and also keeps track of the maximum number of items that have ever been in the queue at one time. Note that the fact that C++ requires you to go through member functions to create and alter a queue allows you to ensure that these data members are always properly set. Change the stopper script so that it also displays the maximum number of items in the queue.

    b) Change the clerk class so that it records the number of times and total length of time it was asleep (not counting the initial startup time) and alter stopper so that it displays this amount.

    c) Rewrite ssqueue so that the stopping point is given by specifying the number of customers to be served rather than the time of the simulation.

    d) Rewrite ssqueue so that it computes and displays the *average* number of customers waiting in line. This is to be weighted over time. That is, each time the number of customers in the queue changes, multiply the old number by the amount of time since the last change, add it to a running total, and change the 'time of last change' to now. At the end, divide by total time.

    e) Rewrite `ssqueue` to simulate a situation in which there are two servers. Experiment with various waiting strategies:
        i) a single line; each clerk takes from the start of the line. Waking up clerks may be tricky.
        ii) two lines, one for each clerk. The arriving customer chooses the shorter line.
Reasonable values for `meanArrivalTime` and `meanServiceTime` might be 3.0 and 5.0, respectively. (Note also that the clerks might have *different* `meanServiceTimes`. What does that say about where `meanServiceTime` should be declared?)

    f) Rewrite `ssqueue` to have each customer, on arrival, choose a random 'sick of waiting' time. If this time expires and the customer is still waiting in line, the customer should leave the system. The final program should include separate statistics on the number of customers that were successfully served and those who got sick of waiting and left the system.

5. With minor alterations, `ssqueue` can be changed into a simulation of time-shared operating systems. The single server is of course the computer's CPU and the customers are commands, programs, etc., being executed by users. The only difference is that the server serves its program-customer until it is done or until the expiration of a **time slice**. At that time, the customer is put back on the end of the `waitQueue` and the next customer in line is serviced. (This is a very simple **round-robin scheduling algorithm**.) To make the program more realistic, you should also alter the method of choosing service times. Most requests to a time-shared system are very short, relative to the time slice. These include simple things like hitting a carriage return to insert a line of text in an editor or giving a simple command like `cd`. Of course other commands may be quite lengthy, such as running the C++ compiler. To simulate this situation, we could compute service time as follows:

```
serviceTime = (random() < THRESHOLD) ? expRand( 0.1 * TIMESLICE )
                          : expRand( 5 * TIMESLICE );
```

where `THRESHOLD` is perhaps 0.80. You might want to keep track of average of the total wait time of each customer as a percentage of its `serviceTime`.

11. Event-Driven Programming

Most large programs now are written to operate in an **event-driven** mode. That is, instead of the program initiating the action, it sits in a tight loop, waiting for some outside event to respond to. When such an event occurs, the program processes the event in the appropriate way and then goes back to waiting. Examples of such programs are games, word processors and text editors, drawing and painting programs, HyperCard-style applications, and any program running under a Microsoft Windows or Macintosh operating system-style graphical user interface.

To write an event-driven program in C++, we program classes to describe the various objects in the program that respond to events. In section 9.1, we suggested a treatment for programming a windowing environment. Each class will have a `script()` function describing the action performed when an event takes place on that object. (Possible events are 'mouse down', 'drag', etc.) The overall structure of such a program is

```
int running = FALSE;

void main( ... )
{
   initialize;
   while ( running ) {
      wait for an event to occur;
      pass event to script (program) of object
         in which it occurs;
   }
   cleanup;
}
```

Look familiar? You bet it does! The discrete system simulation discussed in the last section is simulating just such a situation. Now an `eventqueue` isn't required, as the program's user will determine what happens next dynamically. His or her action will also determine the value of `nextScene`, which will simply be a description of what event occurred. For example, a mouse click in a button might supply the information that the event was a mouse click at such and such location. The button clicked is determined from the location information and its script is passed the information that `nextScene` = 'button click'. Instead of having a `stopper` class to terminate the main loop, the script for a `QUIT` button or menu item will set `running` to `FALSE`.

Moreover, the simulation in Chapter 6 is exactly the same situation! It looks different because the problem is so simple that only one class is responding to events, so its script was placed in the main program.

NOTE: Insofar as possible, the *only* waiting for an event to occur should take place in the main `while` loop. This makes for a much simpler and usually more correct structure, and gives one a **modeless** program, i.e., one in which the user can cause any event at any time. Most large programs have some situations that are **modal**, i.e., not modeless (such as a special dialog box in which the only acceptable event to click OK). However, the more situations like this you have, the more situations there will be in which the user has to guess what is required next, and may guess wrong. Also, it causes code to be repeated. It is a useful discipline to allow any action by the user to follow any other, as far as possible. It has been the author's experience that it is very difficult to convince students, even advanced ones, to program this way, and that the result is enormous, unwieldy programs that react strangely when used by anyone other than the original programmer(s).

12.   Where to go from here

I have exposed you to what I consider the most important parts of C++. What should you do now? As a guess, the language contains about twice as much as I have presented to you. Perhaps 30% of the remainder is picky details I have tried to shield you from and topics which in my opinion were good ideas gone wrong. The latter includes the previously mentioned (in the footnote on p. 40) const morass, which as I have indicated, has benefits nowhere near the intellectual costs it imposes, and therefore should be avoided.

On the other hand, advanced topics like **templates** and **exception handling** (throw and catch) and a few other things are very powerful and useful.

C++ has become very fashionable lately, so complete books on the subject abound and new ones seem to appear weekly. The originals are by Stroustrup (the inventor of C++) and Lippman, both of which serve better as references than textbooks. The current final word is the book by Ellis and Stroustrup, which doesn't even pretend to be a text.

For applications, perhaps the most fruitful study would be to look at DiLascia's book *Windows* ++, which is an extended example of applying C++ in a typically object-oriented manner — event-driven programming. It is a book-length expansion of my Section 9.1 to the real world of Microsoft Windows. Also Pokorny's rather advanced computer graphics text is a source of example C++ code. For use of C++ with standard compiler-construction tools, look at the paper by Hahne and Sato. See the References for further details.

I end as I started, by encouraging you to experiment. C++, more than any other language I know, calls for it.

Finally, good luck! You will need it, and your persistence will be rewarded.

References

Chung, Kai Lai, *Elementary Probability Theory with Stochastic Processes*, Springer-Verlag, 1974.

DiLascia, Paul, *Windows++: Writing Reusable Windows Code in C++*, Addison-Wesley, 1992.

Ellis, Margaret A., and Bjarne Stroustrup, *The Annotated C++ Reference Manual*, Addison-Wesley, 1990.

Foster, L. S., *C by Discovery*, 2nd ed., Scott/Jones, 1994.

Hahne, Bruce, and Hiroyake Sato, "Using YACC and Lex with C++," ACM SIGPLAN Notices, December 1994, pp. 94-103.

Harbison, Samuel P., and Steele, Guy L., Jr., *C, a Reference Manual*, 2nd ed., Prentice-Hall, 1987.

Jones, William B., *Programming Concepts, A Second Course*, Prentice-Hall, 1982.

Lippman, Stanley B., *C++ Primer*, 2nd ed., Addison-Wesley, 1991.

Pokorny, Cornel K., *Computer Graphics: an object-oriented approach to the art and science*, Franklin, Beedle and Associates, Inc., 1994.

Stroustrup, Bjarne, *The C++ Programming Language*, 2nd. ed., Addison-Wesley, 1991.

Concordance

In this Appendix we will give a table showing where various topics in C are introduced in the following four textbooks:

[F]   Foster, L. S., *C By Discovery*, 2nd ed., Scott/Jones, 1994.

[H&S]   Harbison, Samuel P., and Steele, Guy L. Jr., *C: A Reference Manual,* 2nd ed., Prentice-Hall, 1987.

[K&P]   Kelley, Al, and Pohl, Ira, *A Book On C,* 2nd ed., Benjamin-Cummings, 1990.

[K&R]   Kernighan, Brian W., and Ritchie, Dennis M., *The C Programming Language,* 2nd ed., Prentice-Hall, 1988.

Index

Primary reference pages are shown in boldface.